Spirit Sail

Spirit Sail

✦

A Memoir of Spirituality and Sailing

Nelson Price

iUniverse, Inc.
New York Lincoln Shanghai

Spirit Sail
A Memoir of Spirituality and Sailing

iUniverse books may be ordered through booksellers or by contacting:

iUniverse
2021 Pine Lake Road, Suite 100
Lincoln, NE 68512
www.iuniverse.com
1-800-Authors (1-800-288-4677)

Because of the dynamic nature of the Internet, any Web addresses or links contained in this book may have changed since publication and may no longer be valid.

The views expressed in this work are solely those of the author and do not necessarily reflect the views of the publisher, and the publisher hereby disclaims any responsibility for them.

Cover photo at 200 005.tiff by Jan Lichtenwalter

ISBN: 978-0-595-46327-5 (pbk)
ISBN: 978-0-595-70895-6 (cloth)
ISBN: 978-0-595-90622-2 (ebk)

Printed in the United States of America

*In memory of David, who loved
to sail and who is forever
a part of the ocean he loved—
to Barbara, who tried so hard
to love to sail, and failed—
and to the dozens of other crew
who sailed with me on both
salt and fresh waters.*

Contents

Lost and Found

She was a beautiful boat. Nat Herreshoff's early personal yacht. He designed and built *Clara* in 1887—a 35' double-planked ketch on bent oak frames. Herreshoff was the pre-eminent boat designer and builder of the late 19th and early 20th centuries. He designed and built everything from dinghies to America's Cup racers.

We found her in Los Angeles—three recent college grads and a professor. None of us had sailing experience but we were looking for adventure. Neither did we have much money so we were looking for a boat we could afford. *Clara* more than fit our dream even though she was nearing 65 years of age. Her overall length was 35', her waterline 30', draft 6'6". She would sleep five in a beautiful mahogany finished cabin. She had a cooking range heated by wood, a six-volt electrical system, and a four-cylinder gas engine that would push her through the water at five knots.

We offered the owner $5,000 ($35,000 in today's dollar), subject to a satisfactory marine survey. The owner took us out for an evening sail, a beautiful moonlit night—two hours out, two hours back. We loved it! We were as high as the moonbeams.

We had her hauled; the surveyor looked her over. A survey is done by a professional who goes over the soundness of her hull, the engine, rigging, and sails—noting anything she might need to make her sea-worthy. The next morning he called and said, "I'm surprised you got out and back! Her keel is about ready to drop off!" We were shattered. To repair *Clara* with her double-planked hull would have cost three times our offer. There also was dry rot and wet rot, all repairable, but not on our budget.

We looked for another boat but could find none we could afford. Soon my friends were heading back to grad school or on to new jobs. I headed for a new job, too.

Over fifty years later, I sailed with my friend Bill Winslow on his 19' catboat from Riverhead in the crotch of the north and south forks of Long Island to Newport, Rhode Island, to the wooden boat show. We were wandering through the exhibit tent when I turned a corner and came upon the Taylor & Snediker booth. There, on the back wall, was a designer's drawing of boat named *Clara*! I studied it for several minutes. The sailing rig was a cat yawl, main mast in the bow, not the ketch we had tried to buy. The designer was Herreshoff.

Figure 1 *Clara* under sail in 1888 with Nathanial Greene Herreshoff, designer and builder, at the helm. Used by permission Herreshoff Marine Museum/America's Cup Hall of Fame, Bristol, RI. www.herreshoff.org

I asked, "Did that boat ever have a different sail plan?" The reply was, "Yes, there is evidence that at one time the main mast was just ahead of the cabin trunk." I told him that in the early 50's, I had tried to buy that boat in Los Angeles, that we'd had it hauled and surveyed. He was excited. They were restoring the boat for the Herreshoff Museum in Bristol, RI and there was very little information about the *Clara* during that time period. Did I still have the survey?

I returned home and searched my boat files—but no survey. Several months later I was going through old post-college files—and there it was! I sent it to Taylor & Snediker and it is now with the fully restored *Clara* in the Herreshoff Museum. It raised the "what if" question. What if she had been sound and we had purchased her? Would it have changed the direction of my life? Would I have taken my first post-college job? Would I have met the woman I would marry?

What if?

In retrospect, *Clara* actually did change my life. I had my first real sail on her, and my love affair with sailing budded with *Clara* and blossomed into a lifetime. My lost love, *Clara,* engendered my found love, sailing. I did not know at the time that, as in many love affairs, I had launched on a spiritual journey as well.

Figure 2 The author sitting in the cabin of the restored *Clara* at the Herreshoff Museum. Used by permission Herreshoff Marine Museum/America's Cup Hall of Fame, Bristol, RI. www.herreshoff.org. Photo by William C. Winslow

In the Beginning ...

The love affair started much earlier, when I was 12 years old, sitting on the shore of West Lake Okoboji in northwest Iowa. As a youngster, my family spent summers on this beautiful, blue water lake. I was watching three small sailboats out on the water, sailing effortlessly and gracefully down the lake. I marveled at the mysteriousness of their movement.

Sometimes, when the owners were absent from their summer cottages, my buddy and I would swim out to one of the moored boats. We would sit on the boat, dream of dropping its mooring line, raising the sail, and feeling the boat pick up speed. It was the beginning of my spiritual journey with the water and the sea. A Midwest boy dreaming of sail and oceans and distant shores.

My father was an avid fisherman. He told my older sister and me that we could take the rowboat out by ourselves when we had learned to swim 50 yards. It was not long before the eight and ten-year-old brother and sister were rowing together up and down the lake. We each had a pair of oars. Dad would bet other fishermen that his two kids could beat them rowing—and we usually did.

But I continued to look wistfully at the sailboats on the lake. Their grace. Their ease of movement. Their seemingly effortless and quiet glide across the water. And their momentary franticness as they came about. It was all such a mystery to me. A wonderful mystery. But my dad saw no purpose in a sailboat. After all, what could you do with it except have fun? A fishing boat was much more practical. It was fun *and* it put food on the table. It was there that he unwound and, I suspect, found food for his soul in early morning and late evening times fishing on the water.

A love of the water was one of the most profound and valued gifts my parents gave me.

Pursuing the Dream

The dream went unrealized through my high school and college years. It wasn't until another five years—1957—that I was able to begin to unravel the mystery of sailing. My wife Ann and I lived in Chicago for two years. I found a small boat in a yard on the Chicago River. She was wooden with a canvas-over-wood deck, a cuddy cabin, and a fin keel. We kept her moored in the downtown Loop boat basin. Lake Michigan was where I learned to sail, from trial and error, books and friends.

My work took us to the New York City area in 1966. Several years later and after four children, I began to look for another sailboat. I found her in a boat club north of the Tappan Zee Bridge on the east side of the Hudson River. We were living across the river in Rockland County. The boat was a Dutch Contest 25, solidly built, narrow hull with only sitting headroom. She had a traditional layout with V-berth, head (toilet), hanging closet, sink, ice chest under one of the two settees and a quarter berth. She would sleep five, but very cozily and only with very good friends. The two in the main cabin bunk slept athwart ship, that is, across the cabin starboard to port.

We renamed her *Cygnet*, the baby swan that often is black. The previous owner had changed her hull color from white to black. We cruised with her down the Hudson, around Manhattan, into the East River, through Hell Gate and into Long Island Sound. We ventured to Shelter Island, Block Island, Cutty Hunk, Martha's Vineyard and Nantucket. She was a seaworthy little boat, beautiful in my mind's eye with her wooden spars and black hull.

Preserving the Soul of a Boat

After five years with *Cygnet,* I reluctantly decided to look for another boat. I loved *Cygnet* and the many places she had taken me. There was the camaraderie, the good food, and the days becalmed with cooling swims. There were hard sails, anxious moments, and new friends.

I had discovered the cleansing of the spirit while sailing. Somehow, when I stepped on *Cygnet's* deck, I left all the garbage in my life behind—the stresses of the office and a marriage under duress.

It was like stepping from one world into another. On the boat, everyone was focused on one goal. The captain was in charge, even though crew was consulted on destinations, food likes and dislikes, or changes in plans. Our mission was clear. It was a team effort. There was time for conversation. Every day was different. Normally we did coastal cruising, putting in each night, sometimes after dark and a delightful evening sail. Often we would pile into the dingy and head for port from our anchorage, exploring a new "landfall," having dinner in a restaurant recommended by a passerby.

But the urge for a larger boat was overwhelming. When this urge takes deep root in a sailor, it is almost impossible to extract. I had applied for a job in another city, a job that I wanted very much. The competition was severe, so I decided I would get a larger boat if I didn't get the job. I was setting myself up for a win-win situation, whatever the decision. It was the spring of 1984. I didn't get the job. The boat I'd made an offer on also fell through.

Figure 3 My first seagoing sailboat, a rugged, Dutch-built Contest 25.
Photo by the author.

The next morning, my yacht broker called. Bill was a retired Navy ship's captain, congenial and outgoing. He said, "Nelson, I don't know why I hadn't thought of this before, but we're taking a Dufour 34 in trade for a larger boat. It's up in the Thousand Islands on the St. Lawrence River in Clayton, NY. Why don't you take a ride up and look at her?" It would be a move from a 25-foot boat to a 34-foot boat. Her displacement was almost three times *Cygnet's.*

I replied that I had never even looked at a Dufour because I thought they were out of my reach. But I'd check it out. A friend had a Dufour 27. He swore by it. It was "sound, fast, and sturdy." In fact, his boat had been among many that had been blown onto the rocks by a hurricane—and the Dufour survived the pounding better than others. He thought the price sounded right.

I had a weekend when the family was away. I put Darcy, our dog, in the car and headed up towards Syracuse and Clayton—some 250 miles away. Each time I stopped to walk Darcy, I asked myself, "Why in the world am I going up to see a boat I'm not going to buy?" But I kept on going, becoming more committed to seeing her with each passing mile.

I got keys from her owner and found *Lollipop* (his small children had named her) in a shed in Clayton. She towered high above me, huge compared to *Cygnet.* I climbed aboard, unlocked the washboards and peered inside. Her cabin had standing headroom and then some. She had spacious bunks, large V-berth, chart table, and galley. The cabin was huge compared to *Cygnet.* I took the boat apart and put her back together. I fell in love with her.

As I drove down the interstate that Sunday morning, I figured the finances over and over again. *Cygnet* was the down payment. I could manage the monthly payments! I stopped in Syracuse and called Bill. "OK, Bill, you've got yourself a deal." We set up a time Monday morning to sign and close the deal.

On Monday afternoon, I was in my office when Bill called. He said, "I just realized that I've bought your boat and I've never seen her!" I gave him directions from his Connecticut brokerage office to the boatyard near Stony Point, NY on the west side of the Hudson River. About 4:00 o'clock I got another call from Bill. His voice sounded depressed. I asked, "Bill, did I misrepresent *Cygnet* to you?

His reply was hesitant and a little drawn out, "No," he said, "but I just had a different picture of her in my mind's eye." We talked a little more and I made a decision. I said, "Well, Bill, I don't want to feel I've taken advantage of you or misrepresented *Cygnet* to you every time I get on the Dufour. Why don't you tell your boss that we had a verbal agreement that the deal was subject to your inspection of *Cygnet?*" He wasn't sure, but he said he'd get back to me the next day.

Tuesday morning Bill called. His voice was upbeat. He said, "I've checked with the boss, and he says to go ahead with the deal." My conscience cleared. I had been straightforward and offered him an honorable way out. The integrity of my soul and the soul of the boat were intact. We would not feel guilty each time *Wind Dancer's* sails were raised.

A few days later, after I had delivered *Cygnet* to the broker's dock in Connecticut, Bill called. "She looks better in the water than I remembered." It felt good.

I didn't like the name, *Lollipop.* Somehow it didn't fit my image of the boat. So we took the risk of changing her name (it's supposed to be bad luck to change the name of a boat). It was a family decision. We named her *Wind Dancer,* quite appropriate and unique we thought, but since then we have seen many cousins by the same name. Still, she loves the wind, and her dance is sure and graceful.

My boyhood visions, watching the sailboats from the shore of Lake Okoboji, had become reality. In the process, I had discovered that sailing had a greater dimension. It not only is recreation but it also is re-creation, a refreshment of both the body and the spirit.

Figure 4 *Wind Dancer* in harbor at Cape Ann, MA before one of the most photographed scenes in New England—a red shed with lobster trap floats hanging on the wall. Photo by the author.

Introduction

Each of us finds food for the soul in different places: in work, community service, relationships, intimacy, and the family. We find it in worship, walks in the woods, time alone, time with our significant other, time with our children, reading, meditation, music, art, conversation, and deep sharing.

But many of us run on empty a lot of the time. We search for meaning in work—and become workaholics. We search for meaning in community activity—and become burned out. We search for meaning in sex—and find a thrill for a while and an emptiness in the long haul. We search for meaning in friendship—but find few who have the time to invest in deep, caring relationships. We search for meaning in family—and find the pressure of schedules forcing out quality time.

Often feeding our spirit is elusive. Not until we begin to focus on it do we realize that there is soul nourishment in an experience. We have to focus our vision so we see the many ways our souls are fed. Many writers have helped focus that spirit vision. Several writers helped form the basis for *Spirit Sail:*

"I hear over and over again that people are hungry for a life that is more substantive, has deep value and is spiritual. People are looking for a spiritual life that is intelligent and related to their everyday experience." Thomas Moore

"The Buddha taught lay people the virtue of making the 'seven offerings that cost nothing' ... a compassionate eye, a smiling face, loving words, physical service, a warm heart, a seat, and lodging." Jake Kohno

"Any act of kindness, compassion, humor—making someone chuckle in the day—any time you are letting good flow through you, you are expressing spirituality." Alfie Woodard

What is this thing we call spirituality? Virginia Ramey Mollenkott defines it this way:

"I would define spirituality as the experience of the Sacred within ourselves, within our relationship, and within our entire environment. Spirituality refers to our ways of believing, belonging, and responding to the power and presence of Divin-

ity, Holiness, the Higher Power, the All-Inclusive One who connects us spiritually to one another and the whole ecosystem." Virginia Ramey Mollenkott

Our continuing search is to find nourishment for our souls—to bring balance into our lives. We plant seeds. We fertilize. We water. We let the sun shine in. We watch it grow. And then, surprise, we begin the harvest. It begins to nourish us. And as we are nourished, we find we can share it with others.

While sailing has been my special garden of food for the soul, for you it may be quite different. I invite you to try sailing. But I'm sure that there is soul food in skiing and flying as well as many other activities. Perhaps through my identification of where I find soul nourishment in sailing, you will find nourishment in your activities. The chapters in the book suggest different kinds of soul food found not only on the water but in other places, too.

Three Convictions

There are three additional convictions or reasons for writing this book. A book by Eric Berne, psychiatrist and discoverer/creator/founder of Transactional Analysis, popularized by Berne's *Games People Play* and Thomas Harris's *I'm OK, You're OK,* had a line which has had a profound influence on my life. He said, and since I can't find in which of his many books he made this statement, I may be paraphrasing,

> *"One never knows when a word or a phrase or a sentence will change someone's life."* Eric Berne

I have found this to be true in my life over and over again. Most of the time we probably never know what effect our words have had. But sometimes we do. I was at a colloquium on a college campus and happened to stand behind a new acquaintance in the cafeteria line. I saw that she was alone, as was I, so I asked if she would like to eat lunch together. She agreed. We chatted about various things, I'm sure. I don't remember any of the conversation.

A few months later, we met again at a follow-up session. We had lunch again. She said, "You know, last time when we had lunch I was on the verge of suicide. My husband is alcoholic. I was at my wits end. But after our lunch, I changed my mind."

I think for the most part, I listened. And she healed herself. But she needed me to hear her story, to be non-critical, simply to be there for her. I did not press her for what in our conversation moved her to a different place. I didn't need to know. I didn't need to be on the inside of her pain. It was enough to be involved in her healing.

Another person's words helped change my life. I was in the midst of making a job decision. It was a terrible struggle. I was in a secure position, a job I knew how to do. It was creative and fun with good people with whom to work.

The job I was considering was a start-up cable network—a coalition of faith groups launching a channel that would feature faith-based and spiritual programming. I had been a part of the founding of the channel, secretary of the Board of Trustees, and now was considering becoming president and CEO.

One day I got on the elevator of my office building. Following me was a woman who had announced her retirement. As we ascended, I asked, *"Lois, what are you going to do now that you're retired?"* The elevator stopped and the doors opened. As she exited, she said, *"I've enlisted in the Peace Corps, and I'm going to India."* The doors closed. I didn't have a chance at any follow-up conversation.

As the elevator proceeded up to my floor, I thought, *"If she can take that kind of risk, I can risk a move to this new job."* I made the move and it was one of the most rewarding decisions of my life. I felt fortunate I had not gotten the earlier job. I'd had several years of wonderful sailing. And now this was a job I'd been preparing for my entire career.

Indeed, Eric Berne never knew how profoundly he affected my life. Perhaps you have had similar experiences where you have been affected in very positive ways.

Which leads me to my second conviction. In 1976, Wayne Dyer authored a popular book entitled, *Your Erroneous Zones*. I'm convinced it sold thousands of copies because people misread the title. What they saw was, "Your Erogenous Zones." At least, that was my first take on it. Again, there was one line that struck and stayed with me. He said,

> *"As you look back on your life ... you'll find that you seldom experience regret for anything that you've done. It is what you haven't done that will torment you."*

That insight has helped guide me in many decisions. It helped me accept the job at the cable network. It helped me decide to buy a boat. I've gone more places, visited more friends, lived a fuller, happier life. Yes, in a personal sphere, even to marry vivacious Barbara, my second wife!

The "not-doing" has many regrets. Unfinished business. Friends not visited. Trips to parents postponed until it is too late. Words of love or condolence or forgiveness not spoken. Broken friendships not healed.

This truth was strongly punctuated for me in a therapy group where we were dealing with death and grief. One of the women, who had lost both parents in the recent past, observed with great regret and emotion: *"My father and I were on good terms. When he passed away, there was nothing more I needed to say to him. But my mother and I had unfinished business. We were at odds with each other. I wish we could have resolved those issues before she died. I regret we weren't in a more loving relationship."* Regret for what she had not done.

But there is a more foundational belief that has guided my personal and professional life. It is the Holy Scriptures and the ways they have affected and changed lives. I believe in the power of the word—the spoken, written and filmed word. That belief under girded my years of producing radio, television and film programs that tried to inspire, enlighten, motivate, and inform.

And so I write this book in the hope that some word or phrase will affect your life in a positive way, and that perhaps you will be moved to make a decision, which if you didn't make, you would regret in the future.

This book is for both sailors and non-sailors. For the sailors, my experiences will trigger the memories of spiritual experiences of your own, soul food perhaps unrecognized before for its special nourishment. For the non-sailor, the varieties of food for the soul are found in other places, too. Wherever you are. Wherever you look, perhaps it's a process of simply focusing!

Welcome aboard *Cygnet* and *Wind Dancer* for a spiritual journey, enjoy some food for the soul, and discover your own unrecognized spiritual experiences.

◆   ◆   ◆

Moore, Thomas. www.trinitywallstreet.org. May 1, 2004.

Kohno, Jiko. *Right View, Right Life.* Tokyo: Kosei Publishing, 1998.

Alfre Woodard, quoted on www.spirituality.com. May 1, 2004.

Mollencott, Virginia R. *Sensuous Spirituality.* New York: Crossroad Publishing, 1992.

Berne, Eric. *Games People Play*. New York: Grove Press, 1ᶜ
New York: Grove Press, 1966. *Transactional Analysis in P.*
Grove Press, 1961.

Dyer, Wayne W. *Your Erroneous Zones*. New York: Funk & Wagnall, 1970.

Figure 5 Wind Dancer at Henderson Harbor Yacht Club.
Photo by Earl Wagner.

Awe

"Life is lived by those moments which take our breath away."
Arthur Caliandro

*"Those who contemplate the beauty of the earth find reserves
of strength that will endure as long as life lasts."*
Rachel Carson

*"Imagine you're standing at the rim of the Grand Canyon with a majestic
purple-and-orange sunset blazing across the western sky ...
You are transformed, lifted, in awe."*
Rabbi Noah Weinberg

We were sailing on *Wind Dancer*, my Dufour 34, from Provincetown, MA. to Cutty Hunk Island. We crossed Cape Cod Bay to the Cape Cod Canal. Our passage through the canal was fast and exhilarating. The wind was from the Northwest, a beam reach; the current was running strongly with us. Boats must be under power in the canal and we were power sailing with engine and sails, moving at 11 knots over the bottom.

As we exited the canal into Buzzards Bay, it was early evening. The skies were clear with clouds rimming each horizon. Overhead clouds capped the sky like a Jewish yarmulke. We fell off the wind to a more southerly course, the offshore wind on our starboard stern quarter. Power was off. The 20-knot wind kept us moving at hull speed, about 6.5 knots.

As the sun set, the western skies lit up in brilliant reds, oranges and yellows. It was spectacular! We would sail a few minutes, then look again, almost unbelieving the brilliance and color, the beauty that lit up the sky. It seemed to last extraordinarily long.

Slowly the sun sank below the horizon. In the middle of the bay, we could see every horizon: east, west, north, and south. There was color all around us—everywhere. In the west, beautiful yellows and reds and oranges. The east, blues and grays with a touch of pink. In the north and south, more muted, delicate colors.

Then we looked overhead. The sun caught the clouds immediately above us with subtle colors of pink and orange and blue.

There was a hush on the boat. We listened to the water rushing by the hull. We felt the smooth movement as we rose and fell gently in the rising waves. It was as if we were sailing in the nave of a giant cathedral, stained glass sunsets all around us, even over our heads. I have visited many U.S. and European cathedrals. Notre Dame in Paris, St. John the Divine in New York, Westminster Abbey and St. Paul's Cathedral in London. None was as spectacular.

We each said silent prayers of thanksgiving for the grandeur of God's cathedral. It was the most awe-some sunset I have ever seen. It was a sailor's soul food, available only to those few who could see all horizons.

Every sunset is different. The sky changes slowly. Another sunset had fire-red clouds. As a hole appeared, rimmed like the glowing coals of a charcoal fire, one wanted to thrust marshmallows or hot dogs into the clouds for a celestial banquet. Later, the western sky had the rich colors and texture of an oil painting, while to the north the colors blended into pastels and the smooth texture of a watercolor painting.

Awe touches the soul. It speaks of a grandeur more awesome than one has imagined. It *"takes our breath away."* It returns us to child-like wonder. It helps us to see new possibilities. It helps the spirit to soar, and in soaring, gives us energy and life and enthusiasm. Awe inspires us to higher motives, greater reverence. Awe is God touching our lives.

Living Awe

Wind Dancer felt alive. She was flying her mainsail and spinnaker, the colorful balloon-like sail that flies ahead of the forward stay, pulling like steeds in harnesses. She was heading east by northeast; the wind was from the southwest at 12 knots. She was sailing easily, loping along, feeling her strength. Long Island Sound was almost flat with one-foot waves gently pushing us along.

We left City Island in New York City's Bronx at 10:10 a.m. July 20 on a three-week cruise to Maine. The crew included Bob, executive with the communications unit of the National Council of Churches (and a medical technician and mechanic); Jack, New York City electrician; David, reporter and editor. The morning was hot, hazy and humid. We motored until 1:00 when the wind began to freshen and we hoisted the main and a drifter—a light, full headsail. At 4:15, the drifter came down and the spinnaker went up. *Wind Dancer* moved out, finding her cadence, her rhythm.

Figure 6 Motoring through the Cape Cod Canal with Bob and Lou Cannon. Photo by the author.

We had planned to sail until dark and then put into a port for the night. However, we were moving well, the wind was holding steady and the weather was not threatening. We decided to sail through the night. Dinner was cooked underway but no wine. Alcoholic beverages were reserved for when the anchor was down. It was a beautiful summer evening.

When sailing, David never slept. He enjoyed it too much to waste the joy of sailing in sleep. I went down below about 11:00 p.m. At 12:50 a.m., the wind died. We brought the sagging spinnaker down, bagged her and began motoring.

The night became pitch dark. Clouds moved in and shut out starlight. We monitored our progress on the Loran. It showed us our location and speed, plotted our correct heading, and gave us an estimated time of arrival. We arrived at Plum Gut at 2:35 a.m. The Gut flows between Plum Island, the federal animal research facility, and the point of the north fork of Long Island about 100 miles east of New York City. Currents rush through the gut at four to six knots as water races in or out of Long Island Sound, depending on the flood and ebb tides.

We could see the lighthouse on the tine of the fork, but had to judge the distance between it and the island. Once we made the commitment, it would be difficult to change. The current was running with us and so it would be a fast ride through, but disastrous if we misjudged distances. We checked our Loran position, located us on the chart, drew a line for our course that would keep us well off both points of land and shoals, turned and galloped through. Everyone tensed, waiting to feel the shudder of the keel hitting bottom, but all went well.

We felt the winds stirring as we watched the sun rise ahead of us. We were heading due east. A glorious day ahead. We crossed Narragansett Bay, running with current as the tide ebbed, and then picked up the incoming current as the tide began to flood into Buzzards Bay. The currents and winds cooperated for a fast sail. We arrived at Cutty Hunk at 5:15 p.m.—a terrific start for our sail downeast to Maine.

The sail was a *"long moment that took my breath away."* Sailing through the night, I identified with sailors-of-old on tall ships—both merchant and man-o-war—who stood on their decks and marveled at the night sky, who could feel their ships as though they were living, breathing beings. There was the sense of safety and well being in the care of *Wind Dancer.*

The night sky, the ocean, the wind in the sails, the magnificent sunset—I was *"lifted in awe"* with energy-giving images that are lasting a lifetime.

◆   ◆   ◆

Caliandro, Arthur. *America at Worship*. Sermon on The Hallmark Channel. November, 2003.

Carson, Rachel. *Wisdom Quotes*. Jone Johnson Lewis. 2006. 6 July 2007. (http://www.wisdomquotes.com/cat_beauty.html)

Weinberg, Rabbi Noah. *The Power of Awe*. 6 July 2007. (www.aish.com/spirituality/48ways/way_5_The_Power_of_Awe.asp)

Wonder and Joy

"Joy is the infallible sign of the presence of God in Us."
Leon Bloy

*It is a wholesome and necessary thing for us to turn again to the earth
and in the contemplation of her beauties to know of wonder and humility.*
Rachel Carson

*Whatever else we might do to turn an ordinary trip into an extraordinary
journey that feeds the soul, we first need to bring
a sense of respect, wonder, and reverence to travel itself.*
Joseph Dispenza

*"Then God said, 'Let the waters teem with fish and other life, and let the skies be
filled with birds of every kind.' So God created great sea creatures, every sort
of fish and every kind of bird. And God looked at them
with pleasure, and blessed them all."*
Genesis 1:20

*"If you wish to know the Divine, feel the wind on your face
and the warm sun on your hand."*
Buddha

Whenever I step on *Wind Dancer,* I step into God's natural world and step out of city streets, noise, and created environments. I leave behind television and television ads, automobiles and expressways, office schedules and all land-related responsibilities (well, almost).

God's world is sun and rain, glassy seas and stormy waves. It is warm and cold, dry and wet. It is sunrises and sunsets, skies filled with beautiful cumulus clouds and ominous thunderheads. It is a night sky bright with moon and stars and the smell of the sea. It is favorable and unfavorable winds, some boosting us along directly to our destination, other winds pounding directly at us from the direction of our destination.

Into this vast sea the sailor enters on a small sailboat, a boat that is beautifully designed to embark into God's natural environment, to experience only what a small percentage of us are privileged to know. When a sailboat is in tune and in balance, it has strength and power and grace. It seems eager to test itself, to stretch its sailing wings, to partner with God's natural world. There is a joy that reaches into the soul and recognizes that humankind is part of a wondrous world, and that we are not all powerful. Indeed, humankind is only a small part of it.

God's Wondrous Creatures

It was spring. We were taking *Wind Dancer* from her winter home in Brewerton, NY to her summer mooring in Henderson Harbor in the Northeast corner of Lake Ontario. The previous day we had motored through the Erie and Oswego Canals, dropping 105.5 feet through seven locks.

It had been a beautiful trip. Sunny. Windless. Warm. We saw blue herons wading close to shore, occasionally spreading their huge wings and lifting off the water.

Turkey vultures soared overhead, riding the air currents, hardly moving a wing. Fish would surface in desperate attempts to escape predators. Leaves were budding, that fresh, new green of spring. Life was evident all around us.

We tied up along the Oswego town bulkhead for the night, hoping to be the first in line at the marina the next morning to step (raise) the mast and rig the boat. The mast was lying on crutches along the centerline of the boat to allow us to pass under bridges as we traversed the canals. Oswego was once a major Lake Ontario port with huge grain elevators. Now few lake freighters visit it.

I had gotten up early, brewed a cup of coffee, and was sitting in the cockpit enjoying the new morning. The crew were still in their bunks. It was a beautiful, clear day, hopefully good for a sail across the lake. I watched a fisherman on the other side of the broad river, casting out into the water.

On one of his casts, a seagull swooped down and took the bait. It was hooked! And landed in the water. The fisherman gently and slowly reeled the gull in. There was no fluttering or panic. The gull simply allowed itself to be pulled toward the bulkhead. When the bird was near the bulkhead, floating down river with the current, it flew up onto the sidewalk, but it was still 50 feet away from the fisherman.

Again, the fisherman slowly reeled the gull in, the gull walking along the bulkhead sidewalk. When the two met, the fisherman slowly reached down, picked the gull up, and gently removed the hook. There was no struggling, no sound that I heard.

But suddenly, the sky was dark with hundreds of other seagulls, squawking loudly. Apparently a distress signal had been sent. They at least were going to be there as a sympathy choir. It reminded me of how sometimes, the only thing we can do is "be a presence," to be there for a friend who is suffering loss, or grief, or illness.

The fisherman slowly placed the seagull down on the sidewalk. It took two or three steps, not quite believing it was free, paused and then it took off. I felt a surge of gratitude for a fisherman who treated with respect a bird whom many might consider a scavenger. Within a moment, the sky was clear again. There were no seagulls overhead. I sipped my coffee, in wonderment at God's creation and how even the sea gulls could answer a call of distress. *"And God ... blessed them all."*

Figure 7 Seagulls are scavengers, whether on the beach, in the water, or begging for a handout. Photo by Jan Lichtenwalter

Log, Reef, or??

At first, it looked like a long telephone pole or log with seagulls sitting along its total length. We were motoring on a calm Lake Ontario near Whitby, Canada in late June 2002. Heavy Spring rains and swollen rivers had dumped a lot of debris into the lake. We had encountered numerous large, floating branches. Often there were gulls sitting on them, making them easier to spot.

We were on a two week cruise from Henderson Harbor, NY, in the northeast corner of Lake Ontario, to Niagara-on-the-Lake, a beautiful Canadian town on the Niagara River near the southwestern end of the lake. We had enjoyed a weekend of theatre during the town's Shaw Festival and were now headed east along the Canadian shore.

Two old friends and former media colleagues were with me: George, from Berkeley, with his new digital camera, and Bill, from New York City and a cat boater.

Figure 8 Geese were swimming in single file with one white goose in the center. Photo by George Conklin.

We decided that if it was a log 40-50 feet long, we should report it to the Canadian Coast Guard as a serious hazard to boaters. If hit by a fast moving boat after dark, it could mean loss of life. In addition, we were curious. When we were about a half-mile off, it looked more like a reef. But a quick check of the charts showed no reef.

As we got closer, it became a long line of geese, swimming in single file. There were three geese on each side of a "V" in the lead of about 150 geese. We did not want to break through the line and totally disrupt them, but we did approach more closely. They refused to fly. They simply swam away faster, wings fluttering, and feet paddling wildly.

Then, a surprising thing happened. As we approached, they moved into a tight circle, solid with geese. In the middle was a lone, pure-white goose.

Was she a snow goose? An escaped domestic goose with clipped wings? The queen of the gaggle? As we moved away, they reformed their parade and proceeded on their way, the white goose in the middle of the line.

Figure 9 As we approached, the geese scrambled into a tight circle, with the white goose in the center. Photo by George Conklin.

We marveled at God's creation: full of surprises, full of wonder, and the lessons their behavior has for us. How, even under threat, they would not abandon the white goose. Or their sense of "community," and being there for each other. What instinct of loyalty do they have? Of commitment?

Whales and Dolphins

There is nothing quite so spirit enhancing and joyous as sailing with dolphins. We were sailing in the Gulf Stream off the coast of Florida when six dolphins joined us. Fluffy clouds scuttled across the sky. The breeze was 12-15 knots. The water was warm as we ran with the current. The boat cut through the water, sails full, bow dipping and rising with the waves. The dolphins dove and surfaced in graceful arcs. They seemed to eye us with a smile. What wonderful, friendly creatures! It seemed they wanted so much to communicate with us—and we with them! Friends in God's creation. No impulses to harm the other. Each enjoying the creation to which we were born. Somehow wanting to share it, but from totally different perspectives, different environments, different realities.

Figure 10 Dolphins seem to look you straight in the eye as they dive and resurface. Photo by author.

In Maine, we were sailing from Monhegan Island to the mainland on *Wind Dancer*. Monhegan was early described as the "sleeping whale" with the small island, Manana, nestled next to it as the "nursling." We were surprised to see both dolphins and whales. The dolphins cavorted with us only briefly before taking their leave.

The whales crossed in front of us, dove, surfaced, spouted. The odor of their bad breath was a surprise. Seeing them up so close from a small boat—they were bigger than we were—was awesome. They could have rammed us, smashed us, broken us up—if they chose. Sea tales chronicle whales attacking and sinking boats and ships. One dove as he headed toward us. We waited to feel the lift of the boat as the whale might scrape our keel—or lift up under us, letting the boat drop off its back in an awkward return to the water. But nothing happened, only a few exciting moments as we waited for possible contact.

We were sure they were aware of our presence. But they let us be—in our space, close at hand, perhaps showing off their power and making us aware of our impotence. God's creatures. So majestic. So powerful. So abused by man! Perhaps they had a right to feel vengeance for the years of whaling. For decimating their grandmothers and grandfathers and cousins. For polluting their habitat. And yet, there we were, sharing the same space, each perhaps, respecting the other. Friends and not enemies. Wishing no harm to the other. Each wanting to live in harmony, and a wish from deep inside the spirit that our habitats could be healthier.

A different kind of scene greeted us as we entered the Portland, Maine harbor one summer. It was one of death. The water was covered with floating fish eight to 10 inches long. There were thousands and thousands of them. Red gashes marked most of their bodies. The blues (blue fish) had visited the harbor—not to feed but to ravish, killing wildly and ferociously. What moves them to this kind of barbarism?

I mused on the word, barbarism—and its referral to people and armies that were crude, violent, and ruthless. It was a reminder that human cruelty continues in our world—that humans can become unfeeling, barbaric, and cruel. It is what I consider the unhealthy side of our natures. It is my belief that we as humans can choose to feed the unhealthy in us—or nurture the healthy. We have a choice. In a sense, we are like the computer. Garbage in, garbage out.

Each time we sailed out Long Island Sound from New York City, we passed the lighthouse on Execution Rock, reminding us of the barbarism of war. The lighthouse rests on huge rock outcroppings, rising up to split the channel. Myth proposes that the British chained American prisoners at low tide to iron eye bolts secured in the rock. As the water rushed in towards the East River, it rose, drowning the victims. The barbarism of war demeans all who are involved.

Figure 11 We could almost hear the shouts of the old time whalers when spotting a whale because of our own shouts of excitement. Photo by author.

We can allow bitterness, anger, hate, envy, violence to feed that part of our nature that damages relationships, demeans other persons, in fact, demeans ourselves. Or we can feed our souls that which is health producing, relationship enhancing, good for the whole human race, good for all living things.

Serendipity Happens

John had brought two pairs of blue jeans for the cruise. We were visiting the Royal Canadian Yacht Club on an island in Toronto harbor. The club had a dress code that prohibited blue jeans even on the launch to the mainland and the city. With an explanation of our predicament, John was allowed to break the rule and the custom of the club. We took the club launch to downtown Toronto.

The three of us explored Toronto on foot—John, Pat (his wife) and I. John is a retired Syracuse University professor and Pat is a nurse. It was a hot afternoon and we paused for an ice cream sundae at a sidewalk café. As we surveyed our surroundings, we noticed that Wynton Marsalis and his Lincoln Center Jazz Orchestra was performing that evening.

Figure 12 A part of the fun of cruising is putting into new ports, seeing a city from a different perspective. Downtown Toronto from the National Yacht Club, looking east. Photo by the author.

It was about 4:00 o'clock. We walked across the street to the box office and asked if seats were available. "There are," he said, "but if you wait until 5:00 o'clock they are half price!" We waited!

There are 15 musicians in the orchestra. They were seated in three rows, five across. Marsalis started the first three numbers. Then he retired to the upper tier and others took over. The performance was magnificent.

Each musician is a "star" in his own right and each performed solos during the performance. I was impressed that Marsalis shared the spot light with all the musicians. The music was energizing. The musicians were inspired and having fun. Our feet tapped, our fingers drummed. Our spirits soared. We felt the joy of talent shared.

Nourishing our souls is supporting the healthy in us. It is the example of the geese, and not the bluefish. Music can create *joy* and allow us to know "the presence of God in Us."

◆   ◆   ◆

Bloy, Leon. Quoted in *Life is for Living*. Joan D. Chittister, Benetvision, 2003

Carson, Rachel. *Wisdom Quotes*. Jone Johnson Lewis. 2006. 6 July 2007. (http://www.wisdomquotes.com/cat_beauty.html)

Dispenza, Joseph. "From Jaded Journeying to Trips of Wonder." *Spirituality&Health Magazine,* Spring, (2000).

The Living Bible in The NIV/Living Parallel Bible. Grand Rapids: Zondervan Bible Publishers.

Buddha. Quoted in *Spiritual Literacy*. Frederic and Mary Ann Brussat. New York: Scribner. 1996. p. 121

Figure 13 George Conklin in the Bay of Quinte, Canada. Photo by the author.

Hospitality

*"Hospitality is essential to spiritual practice. It reminds you that you
are part of a greater whole ... Putting others first puts you in the midst
of life without the illusion of being the center of life."*
Rabbi Rami M. Shapiro

*"Do not neglect to show hospitality to strangers,
for thereby some have entertained angels unawares."*
Hebrews 13.1

*"... be kind to parents, and to the near of kin, and the orphans,
and the needy, and to the neighbor of (your) kin,
and the alien neighbor, and the companion in a journey and the wayfarer ..."*
Qur'an 4:6

*"Dignify those who are down on their luck;
you'll feel good—that's what God does.*
Psalm 41:1

For the sailor, who is the stranger? Who are the poor? Who are those down on
their luck?

Hospitality to the stranger is a value expressed in most faiths and by many cultures as an essential spiritual practice. When most of us think of a stranger, we visualize persons we don't know. Those who speak a different language. Those who have different customs, different foods, different ways of worship, or a different skin color.

World cruising sailors experience hospitality by people of many different cultures and traditions. And they have the opportunity to extend hospitality to indigenous and foreign strangers, as well as hospitality to their fellow cruisers from many different lands. Those must be special moments, often creating lasting friendships over time and space.

There is a different kind of stranger for sailboat owners in domestic waters. We are a small minority of the total population. Most people have never been on a sailboat. Sailing is totally strange to them; it is a different world, a sea of mystery. To introduce a newcomer to sailing can be a complete delight.

But not always. I knew I was in trouble when the husband of a couple we had invited to go cruising in the Thousand Islands aboard *Wind Dancer* arrived with four hanging pressed shirts. I had neglected to communicate that our "cruising" was more like camping than sailing on a cruise ship.

After we had anchored in a pretty cove of a Canadian Island, we discovered he also was claustrophobic—the V-berth was intolerable. So we moved them to the main cabin. It too, was too confining. He moved to the cockpit.

One morning, he needed a shower so desperately he rented a motel room. I can appreciate the refreshment of a hot shower after a cold, wet sail—but a swim in the cool, refreshing waters of the St. Lawrence River, where water from all of the Great Lakes is flowing to the ocean, is both refreshing and invigorating. Although it definitely is not hot.

In spite of his idiosyncrasies, we had a wonderful time. We raced through narrow channels, granite walls rising on either side of us, current moving us an additional four knots, moving northeast down the St. Lawrence. We broke bread together at a riverside restaurant. We explored a river town we had not visited before.

Anchored in a quiet island cove and after a satisfying dinner on board, we learned more about his claustrophobia and his need for open space. He had been a prison counselor and was viciously beaten by prisoners in a confined space. I get some of the same feelings when crawling in the tight space of the engine compartment and getting stuck in an uncomfortable position. We shared past histories that helped us understand who and why we are who we are.

There are strangers amongst us even though they may be family, friends or acquaintances. There are facets to every person we know—that we don't know: parts of their personalities or lives or experiences or past history that are foreign to us. And of course, most are strangers to sailing.

Cruising on a small boat—whether it's 22 feet or 52 feet—throws people into a unique environment. Companionship and camaraderie is found in many sports—golfing, fishing, tennis, skiing, hiking, biking, and mountain climbing. But to be on a cruising sailboat is a unique experience.

The crew is living together in a small space. They are eating together. They have a common goal. There must be teamwork to make the cruise successful. There are shared responsibilities. There is the adventure of new ports and new places. Of a new gunk hole, exploring an island. Of facing unanticipated risks. Of being uncomfortable and wet and cold. Or being too hot, becalmed, too many biting flies. There is the charting of routes, the noting of hazards, the tenseness of making of a new port in the dark.

Figure 14 Ice cream is a rarity on *Wind Dancer* because there's no freezer on board. Therefore, the whole half-gallon has to be consumed in one sitting—but it doesn't seem to be a problem. From left Sophie Finlayson-Schueler, Bill Winslow and Jon Boll. Photo by Jean Finlayson-Schueler.

There is an old saying that sailing is either totally boring, pure ecstasy or complete terror. There is a fourth: simply being uncomfortable, whether you are wet and cold, or too hot in stifling, humid heat, or seasick. It is this uncertainty that is a part of the allure of sailing. The sailor is never sure what he or she will face on the water even though forecasts are carefully checked. Nor whether there may be a failure of gear—a blown out sail, batteries too low to start the engine, line tangled in the prop or an unplanned contact with the bottom, hopefully mud and not rock. It is this uncertainty and unexpectedness that also contributes to the camaraderie of the crew.

Bill Richards, my colleague and friend, and I invited three young women from church and work to cruise with us from City Island in New York City to Cutty Hunk in Massachusetts. The third day out we anchored in the Great Salt Pond at Block Island. We had had three delightful days of sailing but the girls were ready for "shore leave" without their captain and first mate. They found a lively restaurant/bar with attractive young people to share stories and get acquainted. Time flew by and they didn't get back to *Wind Dancer* until early in the morning.

We set out that morning on a rather bumpy sea. Bill and I got us underway as the girls slept in—but not for long. Soon they were up, sleepy eyed and groggy. Coffee didn't sound good. In fact, nothing sounded appetizing. Soon they discovered that short nights and hangovers aren't a good mix on rough seas. Each became seasick. By noon they were feeling better. And the experience was a part of the bonding and memories of the cruise.

When living together in a small space, there is time. As Roland Sawyer Barth observes in his booklet, *Cruising Rules: Relationships at Sea*, there is "sufficient time for the 'long version'—of everything" and you don't have to tell the whole story at one time. There is time to come back to it, to explore it further, to tease out the details.

There is time after dinner, sitting in the cockpit, enjoying the sunset, to reminisce. Or to feel the coziness of the main cabin, a glass of wine in hand with the boat at anchor and gently rocking, kerosene lamps flickering. There is time to hear another person's story, to pull aside some of the curtains that have hidden the stranger from us.

Chris, my niece, was cruising with her mother and me on Lake Ontario. She is an organic gardener at her home in Oregon where she shares her crops with whomever wants to come and pick the vegetables. They leave cash in a can at the gate, whatever they feel is appropriate. We learned about an international organization of organic farmers and how volunteers will come and work on the farm for a few days or a few weeks for room and board. It allows young people an inexpensive way to travel the world and introduced Chris' girls to people of other places and cultures.

However, Chris explained that the soil was not good for some green vegetables. She could not grow broccoli or coleslaw! She quickly realized what she said and corrected herself. What she meant, of course, was cabbage. I asked her how spaghetti did in her soil. We had a hearty laugh. We were getting to know each other—uncle and niece—who had not spent significant time together since she was a youngster.

While sailing, we learn about each other's strengths and weaknesses. One of the lessons I learned in sailing was that I could function effectively even when scared. Some crewmembers freeze when faced with crises, unable to move. I remember an instance when a large cruising powerboat failed to give us right of way in a narrow channel. According to the rules of the road, a sailboat has right of way over a powerboat, which can maneuver more easily and quickly. All the powerboat steers-person would have had to do was alter course slightly. And I was depending on that happening. We were crossing the channel; the powerboat was in the channel. If our two boats maintained our courses, we would strike them hard amidships. We had to give way quickly, to change tack and direction, or have a collision! This meant loosening the jib sheet (rope holding the forward sail), turn and allow the jib to cross the bow to the other side of the boat.

I was behind the wheel. I yelled at the crewmember in the cockpit, *"Ready to come about,"* but nothing happened. The crew was paralyzed while watching the oncoming boat, sure of a collision.

I yelled, again, *"Get the sheet (rope) off the winch"* and when I yelled his name, he sprang into action, and we came about. We were running now on parallel courses, just a few yards apart. The powerboat never acknowledged our presence.

In another instance, David was on the forward deck raising the jib sail, a large #1 genoa that lapped 2/3 of the way back towards the stern. However, the fastener was not entirely closed and the halyard, the rope that raises the sail, went flying up to the top of the mast. The only way to get it down was to go up the mast and retrieve it. A rule of the boat is that whoever loses a halyard, retrieves it.

David bravely went up in a boson's chair, being hoisted by the spinnaker halyard (the rope that raises the spinnaker). Foolishly, we did not have a safety line because the jib halyard was up the mast and the main halyard was in use. There was no hesitation in implementing his assignment. The mainsail was still up, preventing him from securing himself by wrapping his legs around the mast. A wave from a wake rocked the boat and the swing at the top of the mast was great. He lost his grip and swung dangerously into the shrouds, risking serious injury. As soon as he was back on deck with the halyard, winds hit us hard. If they had hit 30 seconds earlier, it would have placed him at greater risk. We were lucky, and learned not to go up the mast with main flying. Two kinds of crew: those who spring into action in crises and those who are traumatized by crises. It's good to know who is who.

In more than thirty years of sailing, I have hosted hundreds of persons—for afternoon day sails and short or longer cruises. Most I've known. Others have been strangers when they stepped on board. A few have had severe physical disabilities; an afternoon on the water has been an unusual highlight in their lives.

Ayers, my college debate coach and friend, was one of the four who attempted to buy Herreshoff's yacht, *Clara*. We were sailing on Long Island Sound on *Cygnet*, my 25' boat. Ayers was a fairly hefty man. He played football at Northwestern University and his knees were shot. However, he was an excellent swimmer.

The day was hot, in fact, stifling with little breeze. Sweat trickled down our necks and wetted our shirts. We anchored and went for a swim, sliding over the low railing of the boat, relishing the coolness of the water. We swam away from the boat, around the boat, floated, and swam some more. It was pure delight. Until we came to getting out. Ayers could not get out of the water into *Cygnet*. Roger and I got behind him and pushed and heaved, but with no bottom to push against, our efforts were meager and ineffective.

We were towing an inflatable dingy. Ayers could not lift himself high enough to swing over its tubing side. We were beginning to worry that he was not going to rejoin the crew on board. Finally, with great effort, Roger and I pushed and lifted and rolled him into the dingy. From there Ayers was able to get on his knees and to crawl over the gunnel into the boat. Ayers did not venture into the water again, but it was another unexpected experience while sailing that strengthens the bonds of friendship and in retrospect, even had a humorous note.

Sailing requires a commitment of time. Less than a full afternoon is hardly worth the trip to the yacht club or marina. Loading, briefing the new crew, and getting under sail takes time. And the reverse occurs on the return.

There are those who will drop everything, change schedules, desert their wives or husbands to go sailing. For others, schedules get in the way. It's not a high priority. Some skippers, after three refused invitations, move on to other crews. When persons don't choose to go, there is disappointment in not having the opportunity to get to get to know them better, and to share my *"home on the water."*

There are some who are grateful to get off and don't want to step foot on a sailboat again. Some are simply frightened by the heeling of the boat. It feels as though it's going to capsize. Others get seasick. Some find it too boring. Or too harrowing. Sailing is not for everyone, I've discovered.

On one fourth of July, we were weathered in at the docks in Cape Vincent, N.Y., the first harbor on the U.S. side of the St. Lawrence as you exit Lake Ontario. Winds were blustery, gusting to 35 or 40 knots. As evening fell, the winds subsided and preparations for the fire works show proceeded. The display was to be launched from the sea wall that runs parallel to the land. Our neighbors, a couple on a 36' trawler (a power boat designed for heavy weather), invited us over to view the fireworks from their forward deck. The fire works display was spectacular—but the simple act of hospitality created a warm and friendly feeling. The next morning, they proceeded down river to the ocean. We headed into the islands.

My faith and tradition propose to us that we be host to the stranger and to the poor. We discover that strangers can be among the people in our circle of friends and even members of our family. For those of us privileged to own sailboats, the poor may be those who have not had the experience of sailing.

The rewards of hospitality are rich. We get to know persons more intimately and genuinely. We live together, eat together, and play together. We share both our stories and their stories. We share our spiritual journeys. We provide them an enriching experience they would not otherwise have. But perhaps the greatest reward is the long lasting friendships that are so often created.

◆   ◆   ◆

Shapiro, Rabbi Rami M. *Minyan, Ten Principles for Living a Life of Integrity.* New York: Random House, 1997.

The Bible. Hebrews 13:1. New American Standard Version. NASB/The Message Parallel Bible. Grand Rapids: Zondervan, 2004.

Qur'an 4.36. Inc. Elmhurst, NY: Tahrike Tarsile Qur'an. Sixth U.S. Edition 1990.

Barth, Roland Sawyer. *Cruising Rules: Relationships at Sea.* Alma, Maine:Head Tide Press, 1998.

The Bible. Psalm41:1. The Message version. NASB/The Message Parallel Bible. Grand Rapids: Zondervan, 2004.

Friendship

*"A mirror reflects a man's (person's) face, but what he(she) is
really like is shown by the kind of friends he(she) chooses."*
Proverbs 27:19

*"The greatest love a person can have for his(her) friends is to give his(her) life for
them."*
John 15:13

"… friendship offers the soul intimacy and relatedness."
Thomas Moore

*"Relationships with other people form the spiritual web of our lives,
with crucial strands being marriages, partnerships, family, and friends.
According to many religious traditions, our deepest values
are expressed through these essential bonds."*
Frederic and Mary Ann Brussat

*The life I touch for good or ill will touch another life,
and that in turn another,
until who knows where the trembling stops or
in what far place my touch will be felt.*
Frederick Buechner

Sailing attracts new friends and deepens the relationships with old friends.

We were sailing on Gardener's Bay between Long Island's north fork and Gardener's Island. There were five of us: my college-age daughter Donna, her friend Mary, and a couple I had recently met who loved sailing, Jack and Maryjean. It was the maiden voyage, the shakedown cruise on *Cygnet,* my newly acquired 1965 Contest 25.

We had sailed from Stony Point, NY, down the Hudson River, under the Tappan Zee and George Washington bridges with its little red light house nestled beneath it, around Manhattan, up the East River and out Long Island Sound.

Figure 15 The Little Red Light House under the George Washington Bridge was constructed in 1921, an aid to navigation on the Hudson River. It was made obsolete by construction of the bridge. Photo by the author.

On that beautiful sunny day, I was standing on the short aft deck, leaning against the boom that extended back over the cockpit and deck. The wind was off the starboard bow at about 12 knots. Waves were two feet.

Suddenly, the boom swung out. I tumbled into the water. I was surprised that the water was relatively warm. Even though the main sail was luffing, *Cygnet* was pulling away faster than I could swim. Her jib was still filled with wind. There was confusion in the cockpit. Quickly, Donna grabbed the life ring and with a mighty heave, threw it as hard as she could. But it landed just aft of the boat, many yards away from me and upwind.

My first concern was whether I could swim to the life ring, or whether wind and current would whisk it away. After two strokes, I knew I could. I reached it quickly. Other boats started heading toward us to see if they could help. Then I began "issuing commands" from the water. *"Pull in the boom. Come about!"* They had to manually hold the boom in. They maneuvered *Cygnet* to my side and I climbed back on board.

On inspection, we found that the fitting on the traveler had given way. A replacement was easily installed. A little later, Jack was down below in the cabin. He yelled up, *"Hey Nels, there's a lot of water down here."* I dismissed it, thinking it was a little water splashing around the edge of the floorboards as we heeled, water in the bilge. But he insisted I take a look.

He was right! There was too much water swirling above the floorboards. We fell off the wind, running more with the wind so we weren't heeling as much, got a hand pump and bucket, and began bailing. Too many buckets later, the water was gone and we were underway again. We could find no leaks, no source of the water.

After we got underway, water was filling the bilge again. Upon inspection, I discovered water was overflowing the head (toilet) when we heeled enough to bury the through-hull fitting under water. As we moved through the water, the pressure pushed water back through the hoses into the toilet bowl. With the bowl tipped while heeling, water spilled into the bilge. We sailed into our harbor on Shelter Island without as much heel. On shore, we found a marine store and secured a back valve that would allow water to go out, but not into the boat. The problem was solved. It's what shake down cruises are about—to find any problems with the boat.

But another problem developed as we were bailing and sailing. It was quite rough and bouncy and Maryjean became deathly seasick, a first for her. She thought she had an iron stomach. She had been below reading with no problem. She had fixed food while underway. Nausea and seasickness often occur for persons who are in the cabin where visual information and mind conflict. When we got into the harbor and on dry land, her seasickness quickly receded. She later learned she was pregnant with their first child. The combination of motion and pregnancy conspired to bring on that awful sea phenomenon that makes one fervently wish for a helicopter rescue.

Shakedown cruise, captain overboard, bilge filling with water, pregnant crew member—it was a memorable and fun cruise which bonded us as crew and friends for years to come, both on and off the water. Jack and Maryjean were the first of many friendships that were directly related to sailing—friendships that would not have developed without that common interest. Some were found by the grapevine of sailor talk. Others were friends of friends—persons who loved or simply wanted to experience sailing. And Donna was discovering she loved to sail, too.

Figure 16 Amy Lovinger, professional violinist and first daughter of Jack and Maryjean, enjoys a swim and a shampoo in the fresh water of a Lake Ontario anchorage. Photo by the author.

Sage Advice

One of my first bosses gave me some sage advice. He said, *"Nelson, we pay you to take your vacation—all of it at the same time. The first week you are letting down, getting away from job stresses, worry, thoughts, plans. The second and third weeks you are free of the job—you can spend this time in re-creation. The fourth week you are gearing up to return to work. We need you to come back from vacation refreshed, ready to put your full energy into the job."*

It was advice I heeded most of my career. It allowed for real vacations and cruises. Rarely did one crewmember stay on board for the entire two, three, or four-week cruise. A member would get on and off, requiring ports to which and from which crew could get by train, bus or air. Likely they would get off at a different port than where they boarded. The tough part was the scheduling—to be in those ports on specified dates despite bad weather. For me, it meant a variety of sailing companions and opportunities for deepened friendships, shared lives, and common memories.

Sometimes it meant that crew had to fly or ferry to an island. This was the case when I was hunkered in at Cutty Hunk, the last of the Elizabeth Islands that drop southwest from Cape Cod. A four-seat, single-engine seaplane ferried passengers from Fairhaven on the Massachusetts mainland to the island. The pilot could fly into the small Cuddy Hunk harbor blind folded, he had done it so many times. I often watched him drop out of low fog, perfectly lined up to land in the narrow channel.

On this particular day, Jack was the only passenger. He climbed into the co-pilot seat. The pilot started the engine and let it warm up. And he waited, and waited, and still waited. Finally, Jack asked, *"What are we waiting for?"* The pilot replied, *"I'm just trying to screw up my courage to take off."* It was his wry sense of humor that belied his flying experience and expertise. He would deliver the Sunday paper to an island home by flying low, sweeping past and tossing the paper on the front porch. This kind of wonderful story and experience builds camaraderie and shared memories.

Old Friendships

Sailing cements old friendships, too. My high school and college friend, Roger also spent summers at Lake Okoboji in northwest Iowa. Our families stayed in touch through the years. He was among the first I invited to sail on *Cygnet*. We lived in different cities and so he would fly in, take a train to the boat at the end of Long Island or to New London, or a plane to Martha's Vineyard. We explored many Long Island ports and gunk holes together.

Each sailing experience adds a little more depth and respect to the relationship. Just a couple of examples. We were sailing out of Old Saybrook, Conn., headed across Long Island Sound and through Plum Gut between Orient Point on Long Island and Plum Island, one of the narrow points where the ocean rushes in and out of the Sound. Winds and current can make it a rough passage.

We were about a third of the way across the Sound when thunderheads began rolling over Connecticut from the west. We prepared *Cygnet* for the winds that the storm would bring. Winds can gust 50-60 miles per hour in a thunderstorm, but with no jib and deeply reefed main, we were ready. The winds and heavy down pour came. It moved past us in about 45 minutes. *Cygnet* handled the wind and waves well.

As the storm moved southeast, Long Island disappeared in the heavy rain. We decided to head back to Old Saybrook, which we could see. *Cygnet* had only a compass and binoculars for navigation equipment. We sailed by dead reckoning, plotting our speed, direction, time elapsed, and estimating the effect of current. The best decision was to head for a port we could see.

Figure 17 Jack Lovinger with dinner, a beautiful blue fish. Photo by the author.

Figure 18 Roger Burgess, life-long friend, prepares for the worst. Photo
by the author.

But another storm was building over Connecticut. Again we reefed and prepared. As the second storm hit us, obliterating any evidence of the mainland, we
decided to head towards the first land we could see.

That land was Long Island. We headed for Plum Gut. Current and wind were kind to us, brisk but not vicious. There are three harbors on the end of the north fork of Long Island: the port for the ferry to New London; the port for the ferry to Plum Island, the federal government's secret animal research facility; and a small commercial harbor that caters to smaller fishing boats. Neither of the ferry harbors was open to us. We had been in the third harbor before and enjoyed the marina's good clam chowder and food, and especially its hot shower.

The fishing boat harbor was the third harbor, but we could not spot it. I decided to go into the Plum Gut harbor to ask about it, whether it was still there. As we entered the harbor basin, I was on the tiller, Roger was standing on the bow. A man came running out of the harbor office, waving his arms and shouting, *"You can't come in here! This is a restricted area!"*

I swung the tiller over hard to quickly turn *Cygnet* around to head out of the harbor. Roger was not holding on! He flipped over the side, catching the lifeline under his left arm, hanging on the outside of the bow. Unfortunately, I found the scene hysterically funny. I could not stop laughing and go to the aid of my distressed crew. Fortunately, Roger is an excellent swimmer so even if he dropped into the water, it was not a life-threatening crisis. Quickly others gathered on shore, preparing to assist. However, he swung himself back on board, we got directions, and proceeded to our harbor where the shower, clam chowder and food met our expectations and comforted our wet and cold bodies. He forgave me over a hot cup of coffee as we reviewed our day's adventures.

Many years later, Roger, his wife Donah, and my wife Barbara were sailing on *Wind Dancer*. We had only three days and had sailed from Henderson Harbor into the Thousand Islands for an overnight at a Canadian island national park. The beauty, solitude and quiet were magic. Good food, a hike on the island, a beautiful sunset all contributed to a sense of well-being.

The next day we sailed to Kingston, Ontario, an alive and active Canadian city that once was the country's capital. It has a rich history of trade, ship building, a fort for the war of 1812, and wonderful restaurants and shops. The city has created a large harbor in its downtown section and is a very boater-friendly town. We enjoyed dinner in the garden at one of its famous restaurants, Chez Piggy, located in a back alley and in a former stable.

We had to return on the third day. Roger and Donah had a plane to catch. It's not a good idea to be on a tight schedule when sailing. The weather does not always cooperate. On this day for our return trip to Henderson Harbor, the wind was almost on our bow with waves of three to four feet. It wasn't long after getting out of the St. Lawrence into Lake Ontario that the rough weather began to take its toll. My long time friend had a bad back and was in the cabin lying down, pillows piled around him, trying to find positions that would ease his pain. It wasn't easy in the bouncing and pounding cabin.

Figure 19 Barbara is a competent sailor but it's not her passion. Photo by the author.

Out in the cockpit, Donah and I began to turn green. Neither of us had taken seasick medication before leaving nor eaten breakfast. In our many sails, Donah had never gotten sick. I leaned over the side several times. As the day progressed, the wind and the waves strengthened. Our color didn't improve. Barbara took over the steering. She was the only crew who was not incapacitated. Roger, in the cabin, would wail, *"Oh Nelson, you're going to pay for this!"* referring to the debt I was going to owe the helmsperson. By this time, Barbara had become a competent but not an avid sailor. She steered for seven straight hours. As we neared the east end of the lake, the waves began to subside and the crew began to recover. I took over the steering and gave Barbara a much-needed break. We made the plane schedule but only after a grueling day of sailing.

It was not a "bonding" experience for Barbara and me. She tends to remember the tough or rough or unpleasant experiences on the water. As you can by now surmise, I tend to remember the positive and exhilarating experiences. Nevertheless, it is an experience we all remember, although the third day seems to dominate the memories over the first two days of truly sublime sailing.

Each Fall *Wind Dancer* sails from Henderson Harbor in the northeast corner of Lake Ontario south across the lake to Oswego, NY. Her mast is taken down and laid on crutches fore and aft along the deck to allow her to pass under bridges on the Oswego and Erie Canals to her winter home in Brewerton, NY. There she rests safely inside a huge shed out of wind and snow and ice.

In the spring, the reverse route is taken, going through seven locks to have her mast stepped again in Oswego. At the top of the mast is a wind direction and speed indicator. The wind spins the impellor and information is sent to a dial in the cockpit. One year after remounting it, it didn't register correctly. It seemed to indicate wind was coming from another quadrant. I checked the wiring to be sure the eight color-coded wires were connected to the same colored wires. They were. There were no stray strands of wire touching an adjoining terminal. I was perplexed.

We sailed several days with the malfunctioning direction finder. The wind speed seemed to work ok. Finally I inspected the top of the mast with binoculars. Aha! I had mounted the wind machine upside down! I joked that it was really difficult standing on your head in the cockpit, steering, and reading the wind instrument.

It required going up the mast. My crew was Bill, 86, and my sister Helen, 70. I got into the bosun's chair and attached the jib halyard as the primary line to lift me to the top. The spinnaker halyard was used for safety. Bill winched me up; Helen tended the safety line. A young fellow sailor at the Rochester Yacht Club came over to give a hand on the winch. I wrapped my legs around the mast and helped to ease tension on the hoisting line. Slowly I went to the top—nearly 50 feet above the water, about four stories. The view was wonderful. As boats passed, there was a gentle rocking. At the top, I could not see the fitting but was able to reinstall the wind unit by feel. Down again on the deck, we laughed at my installation error—no great harm but another moment of team effort and completion of a successful mission.

Figure 20 Bill Briggs and Marge Fought, Barbara's mother, help take *Wind Dancer* to her winter home on the Erie Canal in New York State. Photo by the author.

The common experiences of sailing, both good and challenging, can bring friends closer. What are the other characteristics of sailing that so uniquely contribute to deepening the bonds of friendship? There are several. Preparing meals and breaking bread together. Sharing a beautiful sunset or small island cove. Exploring new places on the water and on the land. Living together in a small space. Having one focus, one task. Sailing safely. Making decisions together as to whether to venture out onto an uncertain sea. Charting courses. Confirming landmarks and sea buoys. It all combines to sharing a life together, solving its problems, enjoying its surprises, enduring its unpleasant moments and recognizing the risks. All sports have risks. In sailing, they are shared.

Figure 21 Linda Hanick and Jeff Weber secure a shore line so *Wind Dancer* will not swing on her anchor—and then are off to explore—at a Canadian national island park. Photo by the author.

A New Old Friend

Bill Winslow and I worked in sister agencies and knew each other professionally. We served on boards and committees together, attended professional meetings, and worked on common projects. But we did not become close friends until we started sailing together.

Bill built a 19-foot cat boat from the keel up, including its wooden mast, broad rudder, cabin with bunks, cockpit, and beautiful tiller. He installed a diesel engine. *Phoebe Ann* is gaff rigged (a boom at the bottom and top of the sail) with only one sail. On a cat boat, the mast is located in the bow and the boom extends beyond the stern. She sits low in the water so you can trail your hand over the side. But she has practically no draft and can go places *Wind Dancer* with her six-foot draft cannot go.

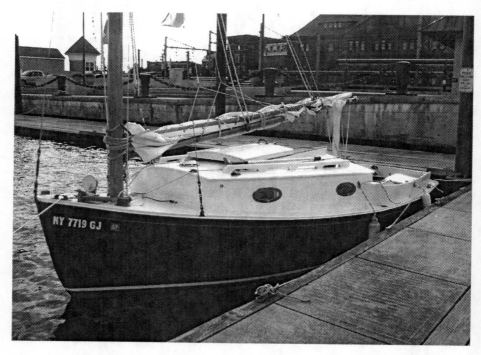

Figure 22 The *Phoebe Ann* was built by Bill Winslow, a sturdy little boat that we sail in coastal waters including Block Island and Newport, RI. Photo by the author.

Each year we cruise for a week on *Wind Dancer* and a week on *Phoebe Ann* out of her homeport in the crotch of the fork of Long Island near Riverhead. Our first night out we were anchored in a quiet cove. A friend of Bill's was joining us for dinner and Bill was preparing a gourmet meal over his alcohol stove.

Suddenly, flames leapt up around the pasta pan. Bill frantically turned the stove knobs with no effect. The flames reached for the wooden cabin roof. The fire extinguisher was by the stove and too close to the flames to reach. Bill could see his boat go up in flames and us swimming for shore. In Bill's words, *"I picked up the flaming stove, carried it out on deck, quickly found a line, tied it and flung it overboard into the water!"*

Swish, sizzle, and the flames were out. That crisis was over but another had just begun. The stove was inoperable so there would be no hot coffee in the morning and for the rest of the cruise—and no hot meals on board. We survived through improvised although sometimes strange meals. However, we couldn't figure out how to serve the red, juicy steaks Bill had brought along. When we got onto Block Island, we found an outdoor charcoal grill at one of the marinas with some leftover charcoal. We stood by the grill, cutting the steaks with our Leatherman knives, and enjoyed the hot, tasty feast. We had forgotten plates and silverware.

Another year we had better luck. We were sailing from Block Island home and passed the stern of a commercial fishing boat. A half dozen beautiful striped bass were swimming on the surface of the water, drunk with too much oxygen from being out of the water too long. They apparently had escaped or been thrown back by the fishing boat. We circled around, I leaned over the rail and grabbed a fish. Bill filleted it for dinner and we had wonderful fish chowder the next day. That year the stove was working fine. And the friendship has deepened as our sailing experiences together increase.

Shared Risks

The shared risks of sailing can deepen relationships.

Four of us were sailing out of Boston harbor on *Wind Dancer*. The crew had sailed together before: Bob, executive, medical technician and excellent mechanic; Lou, his wife, a psychotherapist; and Jan, a media/public relations person. The day was overcast with light fog. We wanted to sail east out of Boston harbor to the Stellwater Banks for some whale watching, then turn southwest to go around the Cape's geographical hook and back into the safety of Provincetown harbor. We hoped to see the hump back whale, the large 40-50 foot mammal that dives with its tail high in the air. They can weigh 75,000 pounds and feed on the wealth of food that is found on the banks. *Wind Dancer* weighs 12,000 pounds, no match for a whale.

Figure 23 Bill Winslow holds our prize catch, not by pole and fishhook but by hand. Photo by the author.

At that time, *Wind Dancer* had minimal navigation equipment. No Loran. No GPS. (Each gives the exact location of the boat.) We had only a knot meter, compass, depth finder and an excellent pair of binoculars. Plus, of course, good charts. We were navigating again by dead reckoning, charting our speed, heading and time, estimating our progress and location, marking our progress on the chart. We also were listening intently for freighters and tugs moving in and out of Boston harbor.

We sailed southeast until 2:00 p.m., looking for the banks where the whales summered. We hoped we might hear or see a whale watching boat we could follow. But didn't. We decided we should abandon the search and head for Provincetown. The weather still was overcast and visibility was about a football field. We had marked our estimated positions on the chart and set our heading for the buoy off Race Point on the tip of the Cape. We continued to chart our estimated positions. We were moving along at six knots.

As we arrived nearer Race Point, the fog thickened. We watched the depth finder to be sure we hadn't miscalculated and were headed into land. The depth finder would alert us to shallowing water. As we proceeded, our confidence in our charting calculations slipped drastically. We became more uncertain and more apprehensive as to where we were. We must have passed Race Point, but we did not see or hear the buoy. Could it be we were outside the Cape entirely, swept out by an ebbing tidal current?

The fog was on the water and did not rise very high into the air. We could see thunderheads forming in the west. We were under full sail: 160% genoa and main and were moving well with winds of 12-15 knots. We knew we needed to shorten sail, but I was waiting until the storm got closer.

Then the winds hit us! They preceded the storm and must have been 10-12 feet above the water. We had been watching the surface of the water and there was no indication winds were coming yet. Sails were cleated down. *Wind Dancer* healed sharply, going over farther and farther. The rail was under water and water was flowing along the deck and into the cockpit. I leapt to loosen the genoa sheet and let the wind out of the sail. Another jumped to the main sheet.

As soon as the sails were released, *Wind Dancer* righted her self. Sails flapped wildly. Seams on the mainsail split. Two crew headed forward to bring in the genoa. Two crew clawed at the main to bring it down and tie it to the boom. We let the boat handle herself for a few minutes; waves were only a couple of feet. The wind continued to blow, with increasing force.

We got the genoa bagged and back into the cockpit locker. We hauled the storm jib forward and hanked her on the stay, changed the blocks, and fed her sheets through them and back to cockpit. The storm jib was raised and sheeted in. She is only a 30% jib. A 100% jib fills the forward triangle between the stay and the mast. Even though the storm jib is very small, we were moving at over six knots. *Wind Dancer* was handling the wind well.

As the storm blew through, the skies cleared. The air was crisp clean. The crew, looking in different directions, almost exclaimed simultaneously: *"There's land!"* In another direction, *"There's land!"* As we looked around, we could see land in every direction. Massachusetts's mainland was west. Cape Cod was south and east. Cape Ann was to the north. We had sailed deep into Cape Cod Sound and now turned northeast to Provincetown.

Jan commented, *"We could have been in the water!"* When we went over so far, it felt like we were standing perpendicular to the water, the boom almost touching the water, and on the cusp of capsize. Fortunately, no one slipped and fell overboard. Unwisely, none of the crew had life jackets or harnesses on. They were going on soon as we prepared for the storm, but it hit us earlier than anticipated. It should be noted that as a sailboat heels, the forces on the boat change. As the sails go farther and farther over, the wind spills out of them and its force decreases. The counter forces on the keel increase. The weight of the keel (4,400 pounds) tries to pull the boat upright through the force of gravity, and the weight of the water on the topside of the keel pushes it down. Nevertheless, keel sailboats sometimes do capsize. Fortunately, we did not have huge waves to help in that process.

We discovered that dental floss was a good substitute when we ran out of sail thread. Lou was the seamstress.

The experience increased our confidence in each other and in the boat. It deepened our friendship by experiencing a potentially disastrous capsize. It made us realize how dependent we are on each other as a sailing crew. No one freaked out. We worked together through the crisis, doing what was necessary, taking what risks were required. Discovering again that we can function effectively through our fears.

A New Friend

I would never have been a part of David's life had it not been for our common interest in sailing. He came from a different world than mine. We both worked in media, he in print, I in television, radio and film. I was separated from my first wife. He was divorced and single. He was ready to go sailing at a moment's notice.

We had many day sails and cruises. One afternoon, four crew left Nantucket Harbor and headed out through the shoal sided channel to the Atlantic Ocean. Again, we were headed to Provincetown, but this time on the outside. We sailed on the ocean side of the Cape Cod peninsula at a depth of 50 feet, steering by depth finder, staying off shore at a consistent distance as the ocean bottom receded evenly into greater depths.

As dusk turned to dark, the stars emerged from hiding. Soon, the North Star was on our bow. There was no artificial, ambient light. We gloried in the wonder of the night sky, the easy movement of *Wind Dancer,* and enjoyed the companionship. Suddenly, there was a whir from the reel of our fishing rod. We were trailing a line, hoping to catch our dinner. We were moving at 6.5 knots so we slowed down to allow the fish to be brought in. She was a real fighter. But in she came. A five or six pound blue. We immediately cleaned her in the cockpit, scaling her in a pail of water to keep the scales from flying all over the cockpit. She was filleted and passed to the galley crew below, who had the vegetables prepared to cook with her—onions, potatoes, carrots—and a variety of seasonings. We ate in the cockpit, under the stars. The offshore breeze gave us a smooth ride. We broke bread together and gave thanks.

Figure 24 David Platt on the wheel heading out to sea. Photo by the author.

David sailed with many different crews on cruises to Block Island, Martha's Vineyard, Marblehead, Portsmouth, Portland and other points in Maine. Portsmouth harbor was special. A performing stage is on the waterfront and we enjoyed musical theater there. The historic district on the water is fascinating. But what we both enjoyed most was an Indian restaurant near the harbor. He was an expert on Indian cuisine and introduced me to some wonderful dishes.

Burial at Sea

In later years, David developed cancer. The summer before he died, we sailed into the Thousand Islands and stayed for several nights at one of the Canadian Island national parks. We dropped an anchor off the bow and backed into the shore, tied lines to iron eyelets driven into the granite, and then pulled the anchor line in to place us about 15 feet from the sheer rock drop off of the island. We swam, snorkeled, and explored the island. He was not strong but game. When a thunderstorm threatened, I took a second anchor out in the dingy and dropped it in deep water off the bow. We did not want to get pushed into the granite shore.

David's cancer was in remission. He had been isolated in his New Hampshire house through the winter. The sun and the water felt good. He was hopeful about his illness, but realistic. He said he would like to have his ashes scattered on the ocean. We talked. I agreed that *Wind Dancer* and I would be honored to participate, but the ocean might not be possible. Perhaps he would be satisfied if his ashes were scattered so that the St. Lawrence River could carry them to the ocean. He had lived in Michigan and the idea that Great Lake's water might carry his ashes seaward was appealing.

The following summer, cancer recurred with a vengeance. His daughter and son were with him. He had communicated to them his wishes. I wrote and assured him that his wishes could be carried out. Soon thereafter, David died.

Barbara, my wife, found several burial-at-sea liturgies and prayers on the Internet. I prepared a service to share with his children. His son, Philip, brought his dad's ashes. We motored out of Henderson Harbor and raised sails. It was a thoughtful time. We shared moments of remembrances. The sail of the previous summer had been the year's highlight for David. I shared sailing episodes. Philip shared some of his relationships with his dad. The tough times and the good times.

When we got to the huge outlet the St Lawrence forms in flowing to the sea, the time had come. We had our service and prayer. The ashes were spread onto the water. They seemed to hang together for an unusually long time, in greens and blues, then began to disperse. We embraced and held each other for a time. We were saying good-bye to a father and a friend.

It was such a privilege to be a part of David's life, to know his daughter and son, to be a part of their lives in this way. We still sail together occasionally, Philip and I.

Friendship is truly "holy" ground, a holy relationship, an intimacy of the soul. The scriptures talk about there being no greater gift than giving one's life for a friend. Most of us don't have the opportunity to literally *"give up"* our lives for another. Yet, each of us chooses how we will *"give our lives"* for our friends, in time, in listening, in caring, in being there when they need us.

◆   ◆   ◆

The Bible. Proverbs 27:19. *The Living Bible. The NIV/Living Parallel Bible.* Grand Rapids: Zondervan, 1982.

The Bible. John 15:13. New International Version. The NIV/Living Parallel Bible. Grand Rapids: Zondervan, 1982.

Moore, Thomas. *Soul Mates, Honoring the Mysteries of Love and Relationship.* New York: HarperPerennial, 1994.

Brussat, Frederic and Mary Ann. *Spiritual Literacy: Reading the Sacred in Everyday Life.* New York: Scribner, 1996.

Bruechner, Frederick. *Wisdom Quotes.* Jone Johnson Lewis. 2006. 11 July 2007. (http://www.wisdomquotes.com/cat_beauty.html)

Gratitude

*"For everything created by God is good, and nothing is to
be rejected, if it is received with gratitude."*
1 Timothy 4:4 American Standard Version

*"I have spent my life teaching our children to say "thank you":
Thank you for the grass. Thank you for the rain. Thank you for the stranger.
Thank you for all the people of the world. I think that if we learn to say 'thank you'
for everything, we will come to realize its value, to respect it, to see it as sacred."*
Native American Chief

*"You say grace before meals. All right. But I say grace before the concert
and the opera, and grace before the play and pantomime,
and grace before I open a book, and grace before sketching,
painting, and swimming, fencing, boxing, walking, playing,
dancing and grace before I dip the pen in ink."*
G. K. Chesterton

The ability to say *"thank you"* from the heart and to receive thanks graciously is a sign of a generous and healthy spirit. When thanking someone, how often do we hear, *"It was nothing"* or *"Don't mention it,"* rather than a simple, *"You're welcome."* For many, it is easier to give than to receive.

It is difficult to give the gift of a "thank you" to someone who will not accept it. There may be several reasons for this seeming "modesty." Perhaps the person has low self-esteem or genuinely feels the gift had little or no value. But for the chronic gift giver who has difficulty accepting help or gifts, there may be more serious issues. Perhaps it is a control issue, or power issue. The ability to accept help, to accept gifts, to be taken care of means giving up control. We no longer are "in charge." The healthy spirit keeps giving and receiving in balance; delighted to give, grateful to receive.

The law of the sea and the custom of the land are different. The hitchhiker has all but disappeared from our roadways. We are afraid to pick up the stranger, afraid of who he or she is and what might happen. Rob us, beat us, murder us. Most of us no longer feel comfortable stopping to help a distressed driver. We are fearful it is a ruse to steal our car or do us bodily harm. Acts of kindness have too great a risk.

Figure 25 Several miles off the Maine coast; we picked up a hitchhiker, who stayed with us for a couple of hours. Photo by the author.

On the water, boaters are expected to come to the aid of another in distress. We recognize that we are in a potentially hostile environment. Around-the-world racers forego winning to rescue a fellow racer whose life is at risk. We are familiar with the heroic efforts made by members of the Coast Guard to rescue boaters at risk. They are chronicled in news reports and movies. We have seen rescue helicopters drop a rescuer into a heaving sea to pull a boater to safety. On the water, an act of kindness for someone in distress is the norm, not the exception.

My first encounter with the Coast Guard as a guardian angel was on the initial voyage of *Wind Dancer*. Four of us had brought her down in early spring from the Thousand Islands, across Lake Ontario and through the Erie Canal to the Hudson River. In Nyack, that crew left and my friend Jack joined me for the trip down the Hudson River, around Manhattan, up the East River and out to City

Island to her summer home. It was a daylong trip but we didn't get started until about noon. I did not anticipate the difficulty we would have in finding diesel fuel. Because it was so early in the season, marinas were not yet open. We had been running the engine a good deal and were planning to secure fuel at marinas further down the river. Each stop ate up time and slowed our progress.

Figure 26 Bill Richards, colleague, and Dara, daughter, crewed on *Wind Dancer's* maiden voyage from Clayton, N.Y. on the St. Lawrence River to City Island, past the Throgs Neck Bridge in the Bronx, New York City. Dara was on her way home for the summer from college in Brockport. Photo by Ben Logan.

We rounded the Battery at the bottom of Manhattan as it grew dark. Rain clouds were gathering. The fuel gauge was showing less than an eighth of a tank. If accurate, that would mean about two gallons of fuel, maybe three hours of running time. As we motored up the East River, we stopped just after 9 p.m. at a marina, but the fuel dock was closed! We pushed on, watching the gas needle slowly drop. Since we were new to the boat, we were not sure how accurate the gauge was, nor certain how far a gallon would take us.

Winds, rain and thunder hit us as we approached Hell Gate, the juncture of the East and Harlem Rivers, a notoriously treacherous stretch with colliding currents. Great whirl pools pushed the bow and the rudder one way and then another. Lightning flashed overhead. Winds gusted, moving into different directions, affected by the canyons of Manhattan's buildings. We powered through, sails tied down. Heading east towards Long Island Sound, we raised the jib, trying to save fuel.

As we approached the Whitestone Bridge, I realized I had not transferred charts from *Cygnet* to *Wind Dancer*. We had good buoy markings under Throgs Neck Bridge, but then had to proceed from memory to our mooring on the west side of City Island. The rain was pouring down. It was pitch black. The wind and tidal current were running with us. We were still under sail.

As we left the East River, we looked for buoy lights. We spotted a light. I thought we should leave it on our port; Jack thought we should leave it on our starboard. A mistake would land us on a sand bar or rocks. I decided. We would leave it on our port.

A few minutes later, we were aground on the sand bar! The current and wind were pushing us on harder. We tried reverse, to no avail. We tried to put our weight out on one side to tip the boat and lift the keel off the bottom. No luck.

Jack stayed above as lookout. I went below to call the Coast Guard. They responded immediately. I reported our location and predicament. Their first question was, *"Are any lives at risk?"* The answer was *"No."* They asked their ritual of questions. How many on board? Size of boat? Life preservers? Are you taking on water? No. It seemed an endless list.

Then came the report. *"We can't come to your rescue unless lives are at risk."* They made several suggestions. Do you have an anchor you can toss off the stern and kedge off? We had no dingy and could not throw an anchor far enough to get enough scope to do any good. There was nothing to be done until the tide rose and currents changed. The Coast Guard told us to check the bilge frequently to see if we were taking on water and to check in with them every 30 minutes.

It was about 11:00 p.m. We went below and heated some clam chowder. The stove warmed the cabin. We put on dry clothes. We could tell from below if the boat moved. We checked frequently to be sure no other boats were approaching, and checked in with the Coast Guard every half hour.

At about 1:00 a.m., we felt the boat begin to stir. She felt lighter, freer. We went up into the cockpit. The wind was shifting from the west to the south. The current was just beginning to run west. Soon we were free. We raised the mainsail and got underway, saving our fuel for maneuvering in the harbor and for picking up our mooring pennant. As we sailed, the wind continue to back, moving to the east. It was perfect. We were heading north. The clouds were gone. The moon was coming out. Visibility was improving. We spotted our navigational buoys and sailed into Eastchester Bay, dropped sails and motored to the mooring.

We called Coast Guard and reported all was well and thanked them for being our guardian angels. They had looked after us, and reassured us they would be there, if needed. We gave thanks, tired, but happy. We were grateful recipients of their gift of readiness.

Jelly Fish

Some seasons, jellyfish grow quite large in Long Island Sound. They may be four, five or six inches across with tentacles trailing several feet below them. They have no propulsion mechanism. They simply float with the current, feeding on very small fish and plankton floating with them in the water. The sting of the jellyfish can be quite severe and very painful. The tentacles wrap around the arms, legs and body, sticking to the body surface, oozing their poison. To some, like a bee sting or snakebite, it can be fatal.

I was sailing alone, returning from Martha's Vineyard to City Island and was monitoring Channel 16, the emergency-calling channel that is monitored by the Coast Guard and by other boaters. I heard a call from the Captain of a powerboat that was anchored in a cove off the Sound.

The captain reported that his wife had been swimming and had encountered jellyfish. She was in great discomfort, the pain was making her nauseous, and she seemed to be getting worse. The Coast Guard went through its seemingly long list of questions. Where are you? How many on the boat? Ages of persons? Life jackets? Boat at risk? Again, the questions seemed to go on and on while this poor woman was suffering great pain. But the protocols had to be followed.

Finally the captain asked again, *"What should I do?"* The Coast Guard replied, *"We don't know."* It was a surprising answer. There was no suggestion that they might call a physician and find out. No solution for the captain.

I had noted the name of the boat. I put *Wind Dancer* on autopilot and went below to the bookshelf to find my medical book. I looked up the antidote to jelly fish stings and radioed the boat. The captain answered. *"Is your wife still in pain?"* I asked. *"Yes, very much so."* I reported the antidote. Rub the affected area with alcohol; it will neutralize the venom. *"Use rubbing alcohol, hard liquor or even wine,"* I said. The captain replied, *"Are you supposed to drink it or rub it on the skin?"* I reassured him, *"On the skin."* I think she got it both ways; he only one.

I was grateful I could help. Two strangers, passing out of sight. Anonymous. A gift given and received.

Rescue

Wind Dancer dropped her anchor between Long Island and Chebeague Island in Casco Bay, Maine, about 6:00 p.m. We were visiting friends on Long Island. While the crew tidied up and prepared dinner, I went ashore to visit a friend and announce our arrival. I was just in time for dessert on the porch overlooking the channel and *Wind Dancer*.

Two additional crew, Bob and Lou, were arriving in Portland and I planned to take the ferry to meet them. My host was entertaining three guests, summer theatre actors, and had to take them to Portland before dark in his outboard runabout. He and his wife offered to pick up our crew. I described the couple and the time they were arriving.

After dinner on *Wind Dancer*, I got busy with some re-wiring in the cabin. Time passed. I began to worry that they had missed each other, or they were late. At 10:00 p.m., they still had not arrived. I finished the wiring and put tools away. At 11:00, the crew on deck reported a boat approaching. I stuck my head out of the hatchway and saw a large inflatable with several men in orange life vests. It could only be the Coast Guard.

The boat pulled up beside *Wind Dancer*. It was the Coast Guard with our crew. Bob and Lou climbed aboard with their gear with heartfelt words of thanks to the Coast Guard. With the disabled boat in tow, the next stop was the island dock to deposit their other two passengers.

We were eager to hear what had happened. They reported they had met each other on time, no problem. Speeding back to Long Island, their engine seized, stopped and would not start. There was no paddle on board. No power, no paddle, no means of propulsion. They leaned over the gunnels and paddled with their hands, the four of them. They were able to make some headway and steer the boat towards an island. Reaching some rocks near shore, they climbed onto them, holding the boat's bow line so it wouldn't float away.

The risk of their situation made them a little giddy. There was laughter and joking. People in an island house nearby thought it was simply a happy party. When they discovered it really was a boat in trouble, they called the Coast Guard, which responded immediately. Islanders reported that if the tide had been higher or lower, it would have been very difficult to climb onto the rocks. And if they had missed the island, they would have been swept into open ocean. A disaster narrowly missed!

This umbrella for the sailor—the Coast Guard and other sailors' willingness and even obligation to come to another boater's aid—gives one a sense of security and gratitude. Often, boats going to a rescue put themselves at risk. Nevertheless, they try. This was the case for an incident in Buzzards Bay.

Wind Dancer had been anchored overnight in a channel between two of the Elizabeth Islands. The islands separate Vineyard Sound from Buzzards Bay. We could choose which bay to sail west in depending on currents and winds. Buzzards Bay was favorable. The wind was strong, 20 plus knots from the north by northwest. Waves build up quickly in the relatively shallow Bay. Fortunately, we were running with the waves. Wind was off our stern starboard quarter.

I turned the radio on to monitor any emergency situations and to keep track of other boats in our vicinity. After about an hour of sailing, we heard an emergency call. A pleasure cabin cruiser had anchored near the Massachusetts shore. Its captain was incapacitated. The first transmission was from him, requesting aid, and reporting his illness.

Figure 27 The author checking charts and locations. Photo by Barbara Fought.

Subsequent transmissions came from one of the women on board. Her voice was desperate, tremulous. *"Please, please,"* she said. *"Someone come help us. The captain has heart problems and is ill. There are three couples on board. We all are in our 70s. And only the captain knows how to operate the boat!"*

I checked the charts and located where they were anchored. They were to windward of us, a tough beat against wind and waves. Furthermore, with only two of us on board and only one of us who knew how to handle the boat in these wind and wave conditions, it was not an option. But we continued to listen as we moved southwest and further and further from them.

A sheriff's boat was dispatched out of the Cape Cod Canal harbor. A workboat on its way to repair another vessel diverted to the anchored yacht. A third boat moved out of Newport, RI. Rescue was on the way!

The woman came on frequently, pleading for help. She was assured help was on the way. Their radio was patched into land lines and connected with the captain's heart specialist. Advice was given. The sheriff's boat radioed that the waves were too much, they were turning back. Sea conditions were too risky. The other two boats proceeded towards the stricken vessel.

Another radio transmission from the distressed boat: *"I see a boat, I see a boat! Please, please God. Let it be coming to help us!"* We heard the two boats conversing: how would they transfer crew to the distressed boat in the tossing, violent sea. They had to be extremely careful that the rescuing boat and the anchored yacht did not crash into each other if out of sync in the rolling waves. It was a tricky maneuver. As we moved further away, we lost radio contact. We were grateful people were there to go to their rescue. I regretted we could only listen to the real-life drama.

However, I discovered later that Barbara was having an entirely different experience. She was terrified! Her imagination was vivid. There were only the two of us sailing. She played out a similar scenario for us. What would she do if I became incapacitated, or fell overboard? She did not know how to affect a rescue. She did not feel competent to handle the boat in the rough water, or to change sails by herself. She felt helpless and vulnerable. She was so distraught that when we got into Pt. Judith, she checked to see if there was a way to leave by train or bus. There was neither. Brave woman that she is, she stayed on board for the return trip to City Island. Sailing lessons began more seriously. The captain was reminded again how important communication is on board.

Wind Dancer has been on the receiving end of the generosity of other boaters several times. One time we were motoring into the yacht harbor at Oswego, N.Y. on Lake Ontario. We edged too close to the side of the channel and ran aground in very sticky mud. We tried reverse, rocking the boat, hiking out on the boom—all to no avail. We hailed a powerful runabout going into the harbor. He immediately stopped and came up beside us, not requiring the depth of water that we did. We handed him a strong line and he gently pulled us free. Rarely will a boater ignore a request for help. We waved our thanks and continued, being careful to stay in the middle of the channel!

In another instance, we had ventured into the gunk hole at Port Jefferson, Long Island. It's just to port after passing through the entrance channel and in the northeast corner of the harbor. The channel is narrow and not too deep, with deeper water inside. *Wind Dancer* draws six feet. The tide was dropping when we exited the next morning—and we touched bottom, coming to a halt. We were a little too late and the tide wouldn't wait. It would only get worse as the tide went out. Fishermen were on the shore just a few feet away. We threw them the spinnaker halyard that leads off the top of the mast. Three persons grabbed it, backed away from the water to give them more leverage, and pulled. The boat heeled, the keel lifted off the bottom, I put the throttle in forward, and the fishermen walked us to deeper water at the end of the channel.

There is so much to be grateful for while sailing. As the Native American Chief said to the Washington D.C. conference (see above), we just keep saying "thank you." Thank you to the people who rescue us. Thank you to the Creator for the beauty of creation. Thank you for the friends who sail with us, for the good food, for deep sleep and rest. Sailing provides the opportunity for a constant stream of "thank you's— *"For everything created by God is good and ... it is received with gratitude."* And the spirit is refreshed.

◆   ◆   ◆

The Bible. *New American Standard Bible.* Chicago: Moody Press. 1973.

Chittester, Joan D. *Life is for Living.* Erie: Benetvision, 2003. Native American Chief quoted in comments to Washington, D.C. conference.

Chesterton, G. K. quoted in *Different Seasons* by Dale Turner, New York: High Tide Press, 1998.

Excitement

"My general formula for my students is 'Follow your bliss.'
Find where it is, and don't be afraid to follow it."
Joseph Campbell

"We have, sometimes deep down, a yearning for <u>real</u> excitement."
Tom McGinnis

Our souls seem to yearn for excitement. Many paths to the spirit are quiet, meditative, looking inward, listening. Yet there are times when our spirits shout for joy, our energy bursts with vitality, our bodies want to dance in ways that are strange to us.

Excitement that feeds our souls is life giving, life enhancing. It is good for our bodies, making them healthier and stronger. There is the excitement of sport activity, of team play, and of individual accomplishment. There is the excitement that challenges our minds, expanding them, exploding in new discoveries and new ideas. There is the excitement we feel from music, art, learning, new discoveries, new places, and new friends. There is the excitement of marriage and love and passion. Positive excitement that feeds our souls.

There also is excitement that is life threatening, life harming, and life diminishing. War, sports like boxing, speeding boats and speeding cars in unsafe situations, gambling, drugs, criminal activities, or extra-marital affairs. That kind of excitement can diminish us and can eat into our souls.

There may be excitement in our vocations and their challenges to serve others, to create a healthier society and healthier individuals, to bring peace to our families, communities and world. We may have a passion to confront injustice and feel the exhilaration of making life better for others. All work that contributes to the betterment of society and the enhancement of the lives of others can be following our bliss and can be exciting.

There are the vicarious excitements we experience at sporting events, movies and television, musical performances and theater. However, too much observational excitement may contribute to the sedentary life style that creates an over weight population and a physically inactive life-style with all its negative health hazards. When these events inspire us to move into new activities, visit new places, undertake new sports, inspire us to find and act upon our bliss, then the vicarious experience can be health enhancing.

When lives and work are dull and boring, our "bliss" may be so deeply buried that we don't know it exists. Or when lives are too full of activity, our bliss also may be buried. When we find our bliss, excitement follows. We are following our dream. We are cutting loose from the secure and the known. We are on a journey of discovery that creates energy, passion, and single mindedness.

Sailing is a health enhancing food for the soul. It is doing, not observing. While sailing, one never stops learning. On every cruise, one learns more about the boat and its idiosyncrasies, more about the sea and its moods, more about the art of sailing. It is locating the position of the boat in fog, or making a harbor in adverse conditions. It is a journey into friendship. Sometimes it is physically challenging. At other times it is dealing with sheer boredom. It often is a journey of self-discovery.

Figure 28 Daughter Debbie Siew and husband, Steve. Photo by the author.

Sailing is food for the soul when the wind blows the cobwebs from the confusion of our daily lives. When the sun dries out the boredom of sameness and allows excitement to enter. When the wind and the sea and the boat and the crew are in synchronous harmony and the boat seems to become a living, driving being that relishes who she is and where she is.

It is then that the sailor's soul soars—and he or she shouts for joy that all is well. The soul's bliss has been found for that moment.

It was this synchronicity—boat, sea, wind and crew—that characterized a sail from Martha's Vineyard to the Harbor of Refuge at Point Judith, Rhode Island on the west side of Narragansett Bay. The day was clear with fluffy, cumulus clouds moving gracefully across the sky. We were sailing southwest out Vineyard Sound. Wind was from the southeast so we were on a beam reach, the fastest point of sailing.

As we exited Vineyard Sound and entered the open waters of the Atlantic, we encountered large rollers left over from an ocean storm, coming slightly more southward than the wind. The wind was 15-17 knots and we were flying the large genoa and main sails. The rollers were coming at us just forward of the beam (middle of the boat) so that we were riding down them at an angle. *Wind Dancer* was moving in synchronous harmony with wind and waves, like a dancing partner.

The crew was my old college buddy Roger, his wife Donah, their college-age daughter, Candice, and her boyfriend. The young couple was sunning forward on the deck. Donah was below reading. Roger and I were in the cockpit.

When we dropped into the trough of the waves, we could not see other boats. On top of the wave, we could see a boat a mile to windward, but when she dropped into a trough, only the top of her mast was visible. We estimated the rollers at 12-15 feet. Only rarely did one break with roiling white water. They were broad based and high.

It was a fast, roller coaster ride. *Wind Dancer* would race down the front side of a wave, surfing so that I wondered whether the bow would keep going down or would lift up out of the trough. It was my second season with *Wind Dancer* and I was still learning her personality and character and capabilities.

As the rollers increased in size, life jackets were donned and crew retreated from the deck to the cockpit. If the bow were to dip under the water on its downward race, the boat might somersault, throwing crew into the water. The adrenalin flowed. We slowed the boat down slightly by easing sails.

While a clear day, our destination was too distant to see. *Wind Dancer* had minimal navigation equipment at that time: a compass, knot meter, depth finder and good pair of binoculars. We charted our course, estimated current and wind drift, and set our bow on the compass reading for Pt. Judith.

Figure 29 Donah could cook up a gourmet meal in any kind of seas.
Photo by the author.

At first, we spotted the lighthouse. As we moved closer, we could see the entrance. The Harbor of Refuge is a V-shaped sea wall that extends out into the ocean. There are entrances on each side of the V. A channel follows the southwest seawall into the port.

The rollers continued but as we moved west, their direction began to move more eastward. The rollers were moving more to our stern and we were riding down them off our stern quarter. They were still huge. The ride was invigorating. Confidence in *Wind Dancer* had grown. We were comfortable that we were safe in her care.

We approached the harbor entrance, waves still rolling, carrying us at a fast pace. The wind had held steady. After we were committed to the entrance, it suddenly occurred to me that I didn't know how deep the entrance channel is. Stupid mistake! In the trough of the deep rollers, we might hit bottom, hard! Adrenalin was really flowing.

A huge wave pushed us into the entrance. Then we were through. We had not hit. Once in, the water was calm. We sailed in behind the breakwater and dropped anchor. All gave a sigh of relief. It was time to relax, have a glass of wine and some hors d'oeuvres. Give thanks for a safe harbor and a sail that provided enough excitement to satisfy our souls for several days. We checked the entrance depth on the chart. It was 25 feet, plenty of water. Indeed, a harbor of refuge.

Roger and I had an earlier exciting sail on Cygnet, my 25-foot sailboat, when returning from a three-week cruise to our homeport on the Hudson River near Haverstraw, NY. We had sailed west through the East River, passed LaGuardia Airport and turned south past the power plant and the railroad bridge. Hell Gate was just on the other side, the juncture of the Harlem and East Rivers. Mythology proposes that tugboats have gone down during storms in its swirling whirlpools. We entered the juncture with a current of five knots. The water was turbulent. As the bow was caught by a fast moving whirlpool, it would dart from port to starboard. The tiller would surge in my hands as the churning water tried to take control of the boat. It was a short passage, but exciting.

Sailing south on the East River, one can look west along Manhattan's cross street canyons. Winds are totally unpredictable. Gusts sweep around the buildings. Sails have to be adjusted constantly as wind direction changes. The river can be busy with both recreational and commercial traffic. Two tugboats in front of us began to "unfold" their barges, stretching across the river. With current riding with us, we risked being swept into them. We lowered sails and powered up, circling until we had permission from the captain to go between his tug and the barge.

Figure 30 Sailing up the East River of New York City pre 9/11. Photo by
the author.

Traveling around Manhattan is a thrill. There are the bridges and landmark
buildings such as the UN. When we enter New York Harbor, we sight the statue
of Liberty across the water with her uplifted arm. As the tide goes out, the currents in the East River and the Hudson River flow to the sea. When the tide
comes in, the currents reverse, but it goes up the East River, where there is no
natural current, earlier than in the Hudson with its natural down-river current
flow. We discovered we could not sail against the wind and the southbound current of the Hudson River. They kept pushing us back into New York Harbor,
regardless of the number of tacks we made.

On one of our tacks from near the statue towards lower Manhattan, a Navy
destroyer was being escorted by tugs through the harbor to the East River. The
current pushed us back out and we were sailing along the southern tip of the
island, on a collision course with the destroyer. Sailors were standing in dress uniform at attention along each of the bow rails. As we approached, we got a little
too close. Now, after 9/11, Coast Guard boats would be escorting us out of the
area. As we got closer, discipline of the men standing at attention broke. One
after another quickly glanced over his should to see if the small, black sailboat was

going to collide with them. We didn't. We came about and decided to sail in the harbor until the current changed northward in the Hudson.

We started up the Hudson at slack tide when there was no current either way. We were headed toward the George Washington Bridge and Tappan Zee Bridge about 25 miles upriver. As darkness fell, heavy, dark rain clouds approached from the northwest. Winds increased. We were beating into the wind. Current was with us as the tide came in. There are no natural harbors to duck into with that wind direction. With a west wind, a boat can anchor under the high Palisade cliffs. One year we anchored there unaware of 60 knot winds passing overhead. We wanted to reach shelter under Hook Mountain on the west side of the Hudson River three miles north of the Tappan Zee Bridge.

As we came abeam of Piermont south of the bridge, the rain and wind hit us. We were reefed down so *Cygnet* was handling it well. The waves built up quickly as the river broadened. The rain came so heavily that it closed in around us. Visibility was near zero. We stayed out of the main channel with the possibility of tugboats and their long tows. Roger was below fixing hot soup. I was alone in the cockpit.

I struggled with the tiller, holding *Cygnet* on course, keeping an eye on the compass to keep my heading. The rain was warm but uncomfortable as it trickled down inside my slicker. In the darkness, in the rain, with wind howling, a strange calm came over me. I could see only a few feet around me. It was like a cocoon. Warm and close and safe. I felt the strength of *Cygnet,* her seaworthiness, her ability to handle the storm. Sometimes in a situation like this, I felt exhilaration and challenged, sometimes even a little fearful. But this was different. I had passed through the excitement to inner calm, an inner assurance.

Within the violence of the storm, there was this almost peculiar calm. I began to enjoy the heavy rain that beat the waves into submission and calmness. I watched the lightning flash across the sky, lighting the superstructure of the Tappan Zee Bridge for a moment. And then again, lighting our course between the abutments supporting the bridge.

We dropped anchor under the protection of Hook Mountain before midnight, sheltered from the wind that was still howling around and over the mountain. Wet clothes came off and were tossed into the cockpit. Hot chocolate warmed us. We crawled into sleeping bags and slept deeply, warm and safe and dry.

Excitement had fed our souls. God had touched us through sun and wind and rain. Worries, stresses, responsibilities had been washed and blown away. And in the sailing, I had discovered the other side of excitement—a calmness, almost serenity, a sense of well-being. My body was tired and my soul was satisfied. There was a sense of wholeness.

◆   ◆   ◆

Campbell, Joseph. *The Power of Myth*. Apostrophe S. Productions, Ind., and Alfred van der Marck Editions. 1988. p.120.

McGinnis. *More Than Just a Friend*. Prentice-Hall, Inc. Englewood Cliffs, NJ. 1981. p. 55.

Romance & Love

"Gravitation is not responsible for people falling in love."
Albert Einstein

"Love and kindness are never wasted. They always make a difference. They bless the one who receives them, and they bless you, the giver."
Barbara DeAngeles

"A kiss is a lovely trick designed by nature to stop speech when words become superfluous."
Ingrid Bergman

"In real love you want the other person's good. In romantic love you want the other person."
Margaret Anderson

It's true! It's not a myth. Sailboats *are* romantic. There is a mystique about them. They are beautiful and graceful under sail. As a person on shore watches sails slowly recede on the horizon, the mind wanders to distant lands, far off ports, and exotic islands. One fantasizes about the people on board and their relationships with each other.

There is a love affair between a sailor and his or her boat. Sailors *fall* in love with their boats. To men, boats are *she,* and they often become mistresses for their male owners. There are several reasons. She has beautiful lines and is full of energy. She's fun to be with and takes care of you in times of crises. She holds you in her arms as you sleep. She is a friend who goes with you into many beautiful and new places.

For a woman, a sailboat has muscle and strength. It is dependable. The boat will do what's asked of it. On board, a woman captain is in command, in charge. The captain makes the final decision. Her boat becomes friend and companion., and submissive to her desires and wishes.

I had a friend who lived with her husband on a sailboat for several years. They cruised, stopped to work on shore to earn enough to cruise again. She reported they had a wonderful relationship—on the boat. When they decided they needed to return to landside life, they ran into difficulty. Their goals were too disparate, they quarreled constantly, and their marriage didn't last.

I can only speculate why the marriage worked at sea and not on land. On the boat their goals were in harmony. While there were pressures and problems, they solved them together. Outside obligations did not press in on them. Family responsibilities and relationships were distant. Life on board was relatively simple and uncomplicated.

For other couples, boat life is full of tensions. Living space is too small. Relationships are too limited. Problems become crises, not only for the boat but also for the relationship. In the yacht club to which I belong, many wives really don't like to sail. Most sail, but it's not their passion. They do it because they love their husbands and their husbands love to sail.

I don't know why more women don't like to sail. Maybe it's because its a male thing, or too macho. Every cruiser has witnessed the sailing couple coming into a harbor to pick up a mooring. The wife is on the wheel, the husband on the bow. As the boat approaches the mooring, it disappears from sight for the helms person. She must rely on directions from the bow.

"Slow down!" the husband yells. She throttles back. He points to starboard. *"More,"* he shouts. She turns. *"Not so much,"* he screams, waving and pointing to port. She turns. *"You're going too fast."* She slows further. *"You're running over it! Reverse. Reverse! You're going to get the line in the prop!"* And so it goes. Women don't like to be screamed at, especially when there is a harbor full of boats with people watching. Actually, I don't like it either. I try not to yell. Shout sometimes, but not scream. Yelling does not contribute to romance.

Neither of my wives likes to sail. Each made a valiant effort. Ann took a week-long sailing course and learned the basics. She cruised some and did many day sails and overnights. But there were too many white-knuckle times and too much nausea. Pleasant sails never outweighed the scary or uncomfortable times.

Barbara sailed hundreds of miles with me for several years, both on the ocean and on Lake Ontario. I was blind to her dislike for sailing. It often made her nauseous and sometimes sea-sick, but she also was frightened of the water, of the boat capsizing, of the captain going overboard and leaving her alone, and of other ships coming out of the fog to smash into us. It wasn't that she was trying to fool me; rather, because of her love for me, she was trying to please me. She was trying to *like* sailing because I love it so much and she wanted to share it with me.

Negative experiences do not contribute to romance. I don't know why we males don't understand this. I have pushed the boat and the crew too hard, stayed out too long, gone out when harsh weather proposed a harbor day. It is one thing to be caught in weather and to cope with it; it's another to go out asking for a challenging, rough and wet ride.

Figure 31 Barbara sailed hundreds of miles and became a competent sailor. Photo by the author.

That's my macho confession. But now I want to tell women a secret about you and sailboats. *When you are on a sailboat, you are much more attractive.* You are at your best! It's a mystery but it's true. None of the beauty cosmetics can equal the effect on a woman of a sailboat and sailing.

It is the sun on your skin and the wind in your hair. It's the glow of your body, the curve of your neck, the shape of your legs. It's the ability to see you in your swimsuit, or in your wet suit, every line of your body apparent. It's quiet time at anchor, swim time in a secluded harbor and dinnertime with soft music. It's a closeness of friendship.

Love on a sailboat is special. It is where Barbara said, *"yes"* to my proposal of marriage. Actually, I had proposed so often that I finally said, *"When you are ready, let me know."* We were anchored. The stars were out. We were in the cockpit and I was holding her as we watched the night sky. When she popped the question, I was so surprised I couldn't respond at first. We eloped in the fall. (I hope that was one of her *good* memories on the sailboat.)

Lovemaking is special on a sailboat, too. It's a different environment. You've had a day in the sun and the out-of-doors. You've had some physical activity, changing sails, hauling on lines, and steering. The movement of the boat requires a constant aerobic balancing that uses energy without one realizing it. There often is a happy, tired feeling at the end of the day.

Each time of intimacy is different and special. There is time. It doesn't have to be hurried. Each can enjoy skin touching skin, the smell of the other, sometimes a salty smell and taste, another time the clean smell of soap after a swim. There are the times of closeness, lying together on the forward deck, a dark night, brilliant stars overhead, and an occasional stream of light from a falling star. You experience God's glorious world, moments of intimacy, two souls finding each other.

There are the times of warm coziness in the cabin, snuggled in a doublewide sleeping bag. Rain patters down on the closed hatch overhead, quieting other noises in the harbor. Soft music is playing. There you are, just the two of you. A foghorn sounds in the distance. A boat goes by and sets you gently rocking in its wake. Intimate. Together. At one with each other.

In the book *The Spirituality of Imperfection,* the authors describe spirituality in this way: *"Spirituality transcends the ordinary; and yet, paradoxically, it can be found only in the ordinary. Spirituality is beyond us, and yet it is in everything we do. It is extraordinary and yet it is extraordinarily simple."*

Our human sexuality is a part of our everyday life—the ordinary and the extraordinary! It is a gift from God to be honored, enjoyed and respected. We come together with another person to give and to receive, to feel the spiritual union as well as the sexual union. When we are in a loving relationship, we care deeply about how the experience is for our partner. We do not want to blemish God's gift to us and to our partner in any way.

A sailboat is a special place for romance, love and friendship. It is time apart. It is time to be together. There is time for romance and lovemaking. There is time for soul-to-soul connection. There is the blessing of being able to give—and to receive—love.

◆   ◆   ◆

Einstein, DeAngeles, Bergman, and Anderson quotes are from www. wisdomquotes.com. Jone Johnson Lewis. 2006. 6 July 2007. (http://www. wisdomquotes.com/cat_beauty.html)

Kurtz, Ernest, and Katherine Ketcham. *The Spirituality of Imperfection: Storytelling and the Journey to Wholeness*. New York: Bantam Books., 1994.

Sailing in Solitude

"Loneliness is inner emptiness. Solitude is inner fulfillment."
Richard Foster

"Be still and know that I am God."
Psalm 46:10 King James

"Silence is a special place you must go to regularly. Silence is a grace
that nurtures, heals, reveals, and renews.... Be still and know. Be still. Be."
Frederic and Mary Ann Brussat

"Your sacred space is where you can find yourself again and again."
Joseph Campbell

Not many people think of a sailboat as a sacred space. We think of cathedrals, chapels, and mosques—buildings that are designed and built for worship and meditation. We think of sailboats as escape from the busy-ness—the busi-ness—of life ashore. The busy-ness of work commitments, taking the kids to lit-tle league and music lessons, community and faith involvements, the demands of making a home.

Yet *Wind Dancer* is where I *"find"* and discover myself *"again and again,"* as Joseph Campbell proposes. Onto a sailboat is squeezed so much life. It is a place where friendships are begun and continued, where they grow deeper and into lifetime commitments. It is where we share the excitement and risks of sailing. We prepare food together, live together, explore together. And after dropping anchor, where we share our life stories, our hopes, our dreams. It is where we express our deepest love to our significant other. From the cockpit of *Wind Dancer*, we said goodbye to friend and father as his ashes started their journey to the ocean. We experience the sacred. *Wind Dancer* has become a sacred space.

It is sacred in another way. The creation of human hands, a boat, takes us into God's creation, both its violence and its beauty. We experience the tremendous energy and beauty of a thunderstorm, and the tranquility of an evening sunset. A blue heron takes flight and a huge tuna arches out of the water. Whales surface and dolphins easily outrace us. It has become a sacred conveyance that transports us into the freshness of the natural world. We move from the hectic, stressed pace of shore life to the slower pulse of nature.

Figure 32 Wind Dancer, solitude and a sacred space, anchored in a cove in the Thousand Islands National Park, Canada. Photo by the author.

We also experience the intimate marriage of the human creation, the sailboat, with God's creation, the water and the wind and the waves. We feel the harmony, the vibrant rhythm, the ease with which the sailboat moves through the water. It is "at home" in its natural element.

There is one other factor in a boat's sacred character. At some point, she transcends her origins of designer and builder, and seems to come alive, to develop a personality. She prefers one tack, sailing faster on one as opposed to the other. She enfolds you into her bosom after a cold and wet sail. She seems to have *"soul"* as she fights through crashing waves and strong winds. She *"takes care"* of her crew in all weather conditions. And the crew treats her with respect and generosity in return. It's a love affair.

It is into this sacred space, the sailor finds silence and solitude, important times of spiritual nourishment and renewal. As quoted above, silence *"nurtures, heals, reveals, and renews."* And *"solitude is inner fulfillment."*

Richard Mahler in his book, *Stillness: Daily Gifts of Solitude,* talks about the healing nature of solitude. He states, *"Clinical studies have revealed that even small periods of solitude can improve one's health and well-being by producing sharper memory, less irritability, improved concentration, deeper relaxation, easing of depression, and better sleep."*

Solitude can be found solo sailing or sailing with a crew. I found it one night while sailing in the Gulf Stream off the coast of Georgia. The other crew were below asleep in their bunks. I was on the 11:00 p.m. to 2:00 a.m. watch. The wind and waves were aft, the wind at steady 20 knots with gusts to 25. We were moving under full sail on a ketch rigged, 42-foot boat. The wind, waves and current were all with us, moving us along at a good clip.

As I looked astern at an approaching wave, it seemed to tower above, threatening to break over the stern of the boat, filling the cockpit with water. Miraculously it seemed, the stern lifted from the lowness of the trough to the height of the crest and the wave rolled under us. Occasionally, as I sat at the wheel, water from a breaking wave would give me a warm shower, interrupting my reverie. There was a harmony and cadence to the waves and the sailing of the boat, lifting up on a wave and then riding down its backside. Phosphorescence lighted our bow wave that ran outward away from us.

In the blackness of the water, I wondered about the huge, steel shipping containers that had been lost overboard, floating just under the surface. Over 10,000 containers are reported lost each year. Would we come crashing down on one? Would it hole the hull or be a glancing blow? I reviewed in my mind the procedure for a sinking yacht. The SOS call and its protocols. Reporting our position, the number of crew, how fast we were taking on water, whether we were abandoning ship.

I went over the steps in activating the six-person life raft resting at my feet in the cockpit. After heaving the 85-pound package into the water, a tug on the tether would automatically inflate it. Survival supplies would be on board. We would need to take a radio, GPS, flashlights, EPIRB and the abandon ship bag of supplies. Depending on how much time we had, we would take additional food, flares, water and clothes.

The night was clear but with no moon. Overhead billions of stars lit a cathedral-like sky. City and suburban dwellers never see this sky. The ambient light from thousands of streetlights obscure the brilliance and diversity of the night sky. It's amazing how much light there is and how much one can see at night on the sea. The white of breaking waves is scattered across the water. I marveled at the vastness of creation, of the mystery, at how long ago our human ancestors watched the night skies and plotted with amazing accuracy the movement of the celestial bodies and constellations.

I was reminded of the Haudenosaunee Address of Thanksgiving—the six nation Iroquois Confederacy of northern New York—in which they thank the Earth Mother, the Waters, the Four Winds, the Sun and the Stars, among many other elements of nature.

> *"We give thanks to the Stars who are spread across the sky like jewelry. We see them in the night, helping the Moon to light the darkness and bringing dew to the gardens and growing things. When we travel at night, they guide us home. With our minds gathered together as one, we send greetings and thanks to all the Stars. Now our minds are one."*

Each verse of thanks ends with the phrase, *"Now our minds are one."*

As I moved from thoughts of disaster to thankfulness, I thought of my many blessings. I have a smart and beautiful wife, great kids and grandkids, a nice home, a boat of my own, wonderful friends. For a fleeting moment, I wondered what I was doing out there. And then I moved on and thought about each one, remembering special times. A laugh or smile. Holidays together. Good meals. Playing ball. Times on the boat. A concert or play. It was a time of thoughtfulness and thankfulness, of solitude where the mind and the spirit had time to join each other, to be one and to be whole.

Solo Sailing

Solitude also is found in solo sailing. When sailing alone, I sail more conservatively. I don't push to the edge, trying to get all that I can from the boat. *Wind Dancer* doesn't have roller furling that allows the front head sail to be pulled out fully in light winds and rolled into a smaller sail when winds increase. It works like a window shade. Without roller furling, headsails must be changed by hand, sometimes on a bouncing deck with water washing over the bow as it dips down into the trough of a wave. Hauling down a large sail in a strong wind and heaving sea is dangerous for the solo sailor. It can be a wet and slippery task, the wind can grab the sail or it can go into the water, creating drag and difficulty in getting it back on board and bagged.

Therefore, if winds are forecast to be 12 knots or more, I sail with the main and working jib, a smaller but a "work horse" sail. We move more modestly, but more comfortably. In addition, I wear a harness with a lanyard that I hook onto the boat, especially if I move out of the cockpit onto the deck. This way I don't take the chance that I might be in the water watching *Wind Dancer* sail away. Charts are laid out and available on the chart table in the cabin, immediately by the cockpit. When I get into waters where I need them, the charts will come on deck, laid out on the closed companionway hatch that goes into the cabin. The Loran is turned on at the chart table below in the cabin. Food is planned and easily prepared. A hand held radio is within reach and being monitored so that I may hear any emergency calls, catch Coast Guard broadcasts of sea hazards, or flip to the weather channel for the most recent forecast. Hot coffee is at hand. The am-fm radio is in the cockpit for listening enjoyment. One or two good books have been selected from the boat's modest library.

The crew had left the day before. *Wind Dancer* was in the Great Salt Pond on Block Island, RI, once a fresh water pond but opened to the ocean to create a spacious harbor. I was headed back to New York's City Island through Long Island Sound. The first port was Old Saybrook, CT., a day's sail away. It would put me on a mostly westerly course, going through the Race west of Fishers Island. It is one of three points where water from the ocean enters and exits Long Island Sound. For good progress, I needed to go through The Race with the tidal current, which could reach five or six knots.

I got up early. The day was overcast with an even layer of clouds. Weather radio predicted an unstable day with possible showers. Wind was 12-15 knots for a port beam reach. I ate a hasty breakfast. I decided to venture out. I rigged the working jib while still at anchor, took the sail cover off the main, hooked the halyard to the sail's head for raising, started the engine, put my harness and life jacket on, hoisted the anchor and headed for the harbor channel.

The ocean waves were only two or 2 ½ feet. Wind was as predicted, about 10 knots. I raised sails and shut the engine down, checked heading and turned on the autopilot. We were sailing hands free! I could sit back, enjoy a second cup of coffee, tune to a classical music station, and settle down with a good book. The unstable prediction apparently kept other boats in the harbor. I was totally alone.

I selected Thomas Moore's *Care of the Soul, A Guide for Cultivating Depth and Sacredness in Everyday Life*. It was a good choice for a day of solitude in the everyday life of a sailor. His first chapter got me thinking about sailing as soul nourishing. He said, *"One person might care for the soul by buying or renting a good piece of land, another by selecting an appropriate school or program of study, another by painting his house or his bedroom."* I thought, *"And I might care for the soul by sailing."*

Earlier in the introduction, Moore proposed *"soulfulness"* is tied *"to life in all its particulars—good food, satisfying conversation, genuine friends, and experiences that stay in the memory and touch the heart."* Wow! Moore was describing what I experienced in sailing. I read on—and sailed on.

The day continued to be overcast—not a ray of sunshine poked through. There were no other boats on the water—I really did have solitude. Every few minutes I would interrupt my reading and check to see if there were other boats nearby. The hailing and emergency channel was unusually quiet. Occasionally I'd stretch my legs, go forward and enjoy the easy motion of the boat at the bow, clipping on my tether as I went.

I went through The Race with the current, an easy passage. If wind is blowing against the current, waves can be high, steep and frequent. And slow going. The afternoon went quickly. Good reading and music. The autopilot was handling the steering. When I approached Old Saybrook, the sun dipped below the cloud cover. It was directly on my bow, about 20 degrees above the horizon. While beautiful, it was almost impossible to look ahead. My eyes streamed tears, obscuring my vision. The harbor entrance is a little tricky. It helps to be able to see the buoys that mark shoals and the lighthouses that mark the breakwater walls of the channel. I was having difficulty seeing either. Sunglasses cut down the water glare, but the sun was overwhelmingly bright. I let the sails luff, slowing the boat to about half speed. If I were to go aground, I wanted to do it slowly. The bottom would be hard sand.

With the slower speed, the sun sank below the horizon, my eyes cleared and markers became easily visible. I sailed into the channel and the Connecticut

River. There's a small inlet just past the large marinas with their huge power yachts. The channel into the inlet is narrow and just deep enough to allow *Wind Dancer* to enter without touching the mud bottom. Once inside, there is always an available mooring that visiting boaters are welcome to pick up. It's an easy walk into town from the head of the inlet.

I found a mooring, tied up, and fixed an appetizer. I made my entries into the ship's log and prepared dinner. I decided to stay on board. During the sail, I had a rich feast of music and soul nourishment. I felt an *"inner fulfillment."* Now, my solitude continued. I could see no one else on any of the dozens of sailboats tied to their moorings. The water was placid. There was a silence— *"the grace that nurtures, heals, reveals and renews."* It was a time of being still, of simply being. And it was good.

I reflected on past spiritual experiences, perhaps my first spiritual crises. It came at an early age. My father was a Methodist minister in a small Iowa town. He invited an evangelist to speak to the children of the congregation. It was summer. The talk was on the grassy lawn outside in early evening while there still was daylight. The evangelist had a large easel and sheets of newsprint. He sketched with oversized pieces of colorful chalk as he spoke.

An image began to appear. It was a fiendish devil, eyes flashing, hovering over children below in a fiery hell. Flames licked around their ankles. The small children's arms were up stretched, eyes frantic, appealing for help and rescue. The children were in agony and pain. It was a horrendous scene. I was four; my sister Fran was six.

His final message was, *"Don't tell anyone to 'go to hell,' because it is not they who will go, but you!"* It had never occurred to me to tell anyone to *"go to hell."* In fact, hell was not a part of my childhood education. It was just not in my vocabulary or my awareness, let alone, that children might be sent to hell!

A couple of days later, I became angry with my sister. I don't recall why, but in frustration, I told her to *"go to hell."* In a gleeful, sing song of children, she replied, *"I'm not going to hell; you are!"* I was devastated. I knew it was true. I had succumbed to that awful temptation. I had told my sister to *"go to hell,"* and now I was going, not she. I cried myself to sleep that night. My mother came to comfort me, to find out why I was so distressed, but I could not tell her. My sister knew, but did not say either. The images of the chalk-talk artist danced through my dreams: pleading, crying, frightened children, begging to be rescued. And I on the verge of joining them!

As time went on and I grew into maturity, I realized how sadistic that speech to small children was, and that a loving God does not scare children into obedience or being good. It simply is the wrong motivation by a loving God—or a loving parent. It may work, but it doesn't create a good, healthy relationship. It's very hard to get close to someone you fear. I think that experience was the genesis of my dislike and distrust of the "hell fire and damnation" preachers.

On that idyllic night, stars out, a quiet mooring, my spiritual reminiscing continued. I remembered the pain and trauma of my separation from Ann. It was a mutual decision. Communication had simply broken down. We were no longer connecting with each other.

Sailing was one of the places I found healing and wholeness. It helped me regain my equilibrium and to find balance in my life. It was here that the breezes could sweep clean the cobwebs of my soul. The sun would seem to warm a cold spirit. I could be with my kids in a completely different place, a different environment with different expectations and potential relationships.

There was the open space that seemed to open up the spirit, to allow it time for healing, and to allow me to go back to facing the hard realities of a relationship that was breaking apart. I found the *"inner emptiness of loneliness"* Foster talks about merging into the *"inner fulfillment of solitude."* An inner peace.

I found that inner peace on another solo cruise. I sailed off my mooring in Henderson Harbor for Kinston, Canada, in mid-September, ghosting out of the harbor on 3-4 knot winds. The winds picked up to 7-12 knots out of the south by southeast. As I reached more open water, *Wind Dancer* moved rhythmically and easily.

I settled into cruising routine. I turned the radio to the Canadian Broadcasting Company (CBC) and listened to interviews with principals of a classical concert that evening. It was the opening event for the 15th International Congress on Care of the Terminally Ill to be held in St.Patrick's Basilica in Montreal. Barbara and I had visited the Basilica earlier in the summer and I could visualize the event with symphony, soloists and crowded audience. CBC would broadcast the concert live!

In the radio interview, Dr. Balfour M. Mount, M.D., was asked, *"As a doctor dedicated to healing the living, why do you devote your time to the dying?"* His reply was simple and profound. *"We don't focus on the dying,"* he said. *"We focus on the quality of life."* (In substance, the quotes are accurate—but done from memory.) It is what we all should be focused on, I believe, *"the quality of life."*

Late that afternoon, I tied up at a dock at the Kingston Yacht Club. There was time for dinner before the concert and I walked the short distance to downtown restaurants. Unfortunately, the electric power went out in all the downtown sections. Restaurants had to wait to serve their guests and I was late returning to the boat. I tuned into the concert as the second half was starting. The music was Mozart's Coronation Mass in C Major.

Figure 33 An evening of solitude and music and musing. Photo by the author.

It was a magnificent performance by soloists, choir, and orchestra. The director was the world-renowned Trevor Pinnock. I sat in the cockpit. The evening was warm for September. The moon hung low in the sky, at first sitting on top of a mast, then moving west across other masts that stretched skyward as if trying to touch it. The music soared, too.

As I listened to the music and the night sounds, I thought of my friend who had just died of AIDS. I was with him while his spirit still lingered in his bedroom. Friends gathered. His pastor came and we formed a circle around his bed, holding hands, giving thanks for his life and friendship.

The timing of the mass, my presence at that time, the aloneness of a deserted yacht club, still grieving the loss of a friend—it seemed strangely serendipitous and holy. It was a time of spiritual nourishment and introspection. It was simply a *"time to be."*

◆   ◆   ◆

Mahler, Richard. *Stillness: Daily Gifts of Solitude*. York Beach, Maine: Redwheel/ Weiser, LLC.. 2003

Foster, Richard. *Celebration of Discipline: The Path to Spiritual Growth*. San Franciso: Harper.1978. p 96.

The Bible. Psalm 46:10 Revised Standard Version. New York: Thomas Nelson & Sons, 1952.

Brussat, Frederic and Mary Ann. *Spiritual Literacy: Reading the Sacred in Everyday Life*. Scribner. New York. 1996. p 411

Campbell, Joseph. www.wisdomquotes.com. Jone Johnson Lewis. 2006. (http:// www.wisdomquotes.com/cat_beauty.html)

Mahler, Richard. *Stillness: Daily Gifts of Solitude*. San Francisco: Red Wheel. 2003. Quoted from review by Frederic and Mary Ann Brussat at www. spiritualityhealth.com

Haudenosaunee Address of Thanksgiving. Six Nations Indian Museum and the Tracking Project. 1993

Moore, Thomas. *Care of the Soul: A Guide for Cultivating Depth and Sacredness in Everyday Life*. New York: HarperPerennial, 1994

Sailing in a Sea of Abundance

"Blessed is he who considers the poor;
the Lord delivers him in the day of trouble."
Psalm 41.1

"Be compassionate to orphans and relieve widows.
Respect the old and help the poor."
Taoism. Tract of the Quiet Way

"Charity—to be moved at the sight of the thirsty,
the hungry, and the miserable and to offer
relief to them out of pity—is the spring of virtue."
Jainism. Kundakunda, Pancastikaya 137

"They feed with food the needy wretch, the orphan, and the
prisoner, for love of Him, saying, 'We wish for no
reward nor thanks from you'."
Islam. Qur'an 76.8-9

"Much is required from those to whom much is given."
Luke 12:48

Sailing for pleasure and adventure—even for the nourishment of the soul—is possible only in a society of abundance or by persons of wealth in societies of poverty. Affluence for millions in the United States has been made possible by the huge resources of the land and a people eager to develop them. We have been truly blessed.

Each of the great faiths ask us to be generous to the poor, to help the stranger, to feed the hungry, to take care of the children, and to recognize those who are in desperate situations. How do we justify owning boats in a world where there is so much suffering and injustice? I wrestle with these admonitions in the sacred texts.

We live in a world where war continues and families are ripped apart by death and injury, by psychological devastation and soul wrenching experiences. Where children die of malnutrition and illness. Where families are homeless. Where hundreds of thousands live in refugee camps and millions are sentenced to death by AIDS.

We Americans live in the wealthiest country in the world, yet children have inadequate health care, housing and educational opportunity; where violence rules some neighborhoods and teens are dying at unprecedented rates of murder, suicide and motor vehicle accidents.

It is hard for me to justify the extravagance of the mega yacht, the mega home, the mega car—what is often called "conspicuous consumption." Perhaps it is better recognized as outrageous self-indulgence. Likewise, how does one justify the building of great cathedrals, performance centers, and museums when those resources might be directed to alleviate suffering of so many people in so many places?

Where each individual draws the line is a personal choice measured against personal conscience. Where do our personal welfare and comfort end and our commitment to community and to change for the community and world begin? Where does the "I" change to the "We?"

How does the community decide where to put its resources? Into programs for children and youth to give them healthy options? Into education? Into creating healthier neighborhoods? Into larger prisons? Into tax incentives for mega malls and commercial development? Answers are not easy.

We live in a country where taxes favor the rich and the chasm between rich and poor grows greater. Often all who pay taxes help to underwrite the purchase price of a boat or yacht. If the boat has a head, a galley, and sleeping quarters, it can be classified as a second home. Interest on a loan can be an income tax deduction, thus increasing the tax liability of others.

Corporations own many mega yachts. Their purchase price can be depreciated and their cost of operation deducted as a business expense, thus reducing the company's tax liability. The bigger the yacht and its cost, the more the public pays for it through taxes not paid by the owners. This public support of corporate extravagance or "second homes" for the middle and upper classes, be they yachts, boats, motor homes or, indeed, vacation homes, is difficult to justify when measured against the needs of the poor.

Wind Dancer was docked behind a large trawler, about 42' in length. A trawler is often the next boat of an aging sailor who no longer wants to wrestle with wind and sails. It is spacious and comfortable. But unlike a gasoline-powered yacht, a trawler has a diesel engine. It is dependable. Diesel fuel is safer; its fumes do not gather in the bilge and explode if ignited by spark or stove flame. And it is slower. A trawler cruises at 7-8 knots, as opposed to 35 plus for a gasoline powered yacht.

As we chatted, I asked the owner how often he fueled up. *"Once a year,"* was his reply. Surprise showed on my face. He had just arrived in the north from Florida. *"How large is your tank?"* I asked. *"Seven hundred gallons,"* he said with a smile. I did some quick calculations. If he got about five miles to the gallon, he could travel 3,500 miles on a tank of gas! At $3.00 per gallon, that was a hefty $2,100, but he paid no real estate taxes and lived aboard. The gasoline bill for the average person who drives 15,000 miles per year and averages 30 mpg will be $1,500. He traveled to many ports from south to north, visiting new places, experiencing the different cultures within our country. Perhaps the trade off was not that extravagant.

How do we balance our affluence with our responsibility? This is not a treatise on social ethics or the ethics of abundance. However, each of us must struggle with what is healthy for our souls and what is health producing for the souls of others. I share with you where I am with this 'soul wrenching' issue.

Sharing/Hospitality

First, we share. We share time on the boat and time on the water with others who otherwise would not have this experience. (See chapter on Hospitality.) We go places that only can be reached by boat, sharing a different world.

We share the experience of sailing. The wind in the face. The sun on the back. The boat heeling, cutting through the water. They experience steering the boat, feeling her immediate response to the slightest turn of the wheel. They stand on the bow, letting the wind blow through their hair, listening to the bow wave, riding up and over the waves. I remember how Sophie, about 13 years of age, spent her entire afternoon riding the bow.

They experience swinging on an anchor after a day's sail, taking a dip in the cool water, exploring an island. They enjoy food prepared in the galley, handed up to crew in the cockpit, gathering around the small cockpit table, juggling food and drink, laughter and conversation.

As the night gets darker, they lie on the deck and watch for shooting stars. In the darkness with no ambient light dimming the night sky, they marvel at the vastness and beauty of God's universe. Their souls are nourished and refreshed.

We share ourselves in friendship. One evening, after dark, all were gathered in the cabin. The oil lamps cast a soft glow against the mahogany wood. Wine glasses were half empty. Three couples were seated in the main cabin, four on the

U-shaped settee on the port side, and two on the single bunk on the starboard. The night was calm with a little chill in the air. The cabin was warm and cozy.

The conversation started out with remembering the day of sailing. But quickly it turned to more serious and intimate issues. One of the women was dealing with sex discrimination on the job. Another had a parent dealing with Alzheimer's disease. A job change was in the offing for one of the guys. I was dealing with job pressure and stress. It was a time of letting down pretenses and being real for each other. Listening. Empathizing. An occasional suggestion. But no one trying to solve another's problems. It was a time of closeness, caring and intimacy. As boat owners, we share a space where intimacy can occur, where friendships can deepen, where our spirits can be nourished. We give the gift of our presence.

Giving Back

We are reminded by each of our religious traditions in various ways that *"to whom much is given, much is required."* We are asked to *"give back."* We begin to fulfill this obligation in several ways.

First, by being involved and committed to our church, synagogue, mosque or religious tradition. Each faith tradition is involved in the nourishment of the soul, in community outreach and in opposition to injustice.

It was the Black church that was the primary strength and inspiration for the civil rights movement. The boycott of South Africa to protest apartheid was initiated by the churches of America and England. It was the religious community in England that began the campaign which resulted in the abolition of the slave trade in 1807 by British vessels. Religious organizations have established schools, hospitals, colleges and job training for people in developing countries.

Being involved with and providing financial support for our religious institutions can help to relieve suffering and contribute to making a healthier world.

Secondly, there are the many community organizations working to alleviate suffering through community centers, job training, rape crises centers, day care centers, literacy centers, health providers and counseling centers. All need volunteers.

Third, to change systemic injustice often requires political involvement. Many of the critical oppressive systems cannot be resolved by local community or religious groups. It requires action at the city, state or national government levels. Health care and high drug costs must be dealt with nationally. Others include degradation of our environment, fossil fuel pollution, storage of nuclear waste, clean up of toxic sites, finding ways to keep jobs in the U.S., protecting us from foreign aggression and protecting our environment. We need to be politically involved, supporting those candidates who will resist and oppose special interests, and work for the good of all citizens.

And lastly, there are many national and international organizations that need our support and our voice to speak to our political representatives. Agencies conducting medical research to find cures to disease, environmental protection organizations, educational efforts for public health and safety, and efforts to rescue children from poverty and abuse. We have many opportunities to help secure a healthier society and world home.

As sailors, we can be proud of the fact that we contribute minimum pollution to our environment. Wind is used as the primary "fuel." Raw sewage is not dumped into the water but into holding tanks on the boat, emptied later at shore stations. Unlike automobiles, fiberglass boats last for decades. Sailors appreciate nature and its beauty. We try not to abuse our environment, our earth home.

Vocation

Recently the electricity went out in our community. We were surprised at how much we were dependent upon this single resource. It was less than 10 degrees Fahrenheit outside. The electronic starter did not work to start the furnace. The house began to cool rapidly. We resorted to our wood-burning fireplace. Refrigerator, television, and radios were silent. Clocks stopped. Computers shut down. The garage door would not open without power. We were grateful for the workers who restored electricity within a few hours. I appreciated Jack, my electrician friend, and his "holy" work.

Most working people are in vocations that contribute positively to society. We contribute to a better world through our work. Electricians, plumbers and construction workers contribute to our basic need for shelter. Farmers and agricultural workers contribute to our basic need for safe food. Truck drivers and transportation systems contribute to our access to food and most of the acquired *things* in our lives. People working in our medical systems contribute to our physical health.

My first boss said, *"God calls you where your talents cross human need."* For many, vocation is a sacred calling, a place where they can "pay their dues" for taking up space in this world. They see how their work contributes to a better society, how it positively affects people's lives. In this sense, we contribute through vocations that are health enhancing rather than health threatening, both physically and mentally, both individually and for the world society. Most of us "give back" through our vocations.

Beauty

Poverty and beauty exist side by side. Poverty challenges our social conscience to find ways to end it. Beauty lives to inspire us. It feeds our souls.

To crucify beauty in the name of eliminating poverty would ultimately impoverish all of us. Our souls need beauty to inspire us to see the poverty around us. And to move us to do something about it.

Beauty is an antidote to despair. It is a set of wings on which the soul soars. It comes in many forms. Through the architecture of beautiful buildings, music of the great composers, the improvisation of jazz, paintings, photography, film, drama, dance, and sculpture. Great art in whatever form is a meeting of souls, a deep human connection.

Matthew Fox, in *Original Blessing,* writes:

> *"Beauty saves. Beauty heals. Beauty motivates. Beauty unites. Beauty returns us to our origins, and here lies the ultimate act of saving, of healing, of overcoming dualism. Beauty allows us to forget the pain and dwell on the joy."*

The souls of people of every age have motivated them to create beauty. We think of western art and artists. But civilizations before us created their own art: the Aztecs, Mayans, Greeks, Romans, Africans, and Native Americans—all peoples. Beauty has always been an expression of the soul.

Ralph Waldo Emerson wrote:

> *"Never lose an opportunity of seeing anything that is beautiful; for beauty is God's handwriting."*

Beauty is contagious. It creates a zest for life. It energizes and motivates. It creates a sense of awe at the skill of the creator.

For the sailor, the sailboat also is a creation of beauty: its lines, its grace under sail, and its ability to move into the beauty of God's natural world. There is the beauty of the workmanship in the cabin, everything fitting perfectly, every detail executed for a purpose.

A sailor lives within a creation of beauty and moves into world of beauty. There is the diversity of weather that brings the beauty of a sunset, the magnitude of a thunderstorm, and the quiet of a star lit night. There is the diversity of landscapes, new ports, shorelines, lighthouses, and seascapes.

Beauty is a life-blood of the soul. Somehow we must find a balance between all humankind's need for beauty and its nourishment of the soul, and at the same time, the elimination of the life-threatening needs of the poor and the bloodletting of the soul.

Hospitality, sharing, vocation, giving back through service and continuing to create beauty that inspires the soul and energizes our commitment—these are ways I have found that help me find some peace as a person who lives in a "sea of abundance."

◆   ◆   ◆

The five quotations from various world faiths at the beginning of the chapter were found on www.unification.net/ws/theme141.htm—World Scripture—Charity and Hospitality. 2004

Fox, Matthew. *Original Blessing: A Primer in Creation Spirituality*. Rochester, VT: Bear & Company,1996

Emerson, Ralph Waldo. Quoted in *To See the World in a Grain of Sand*. Edited by Caesar Johnson. C. R. Gibson Company. 1983. Found on www. SpiritualityHealth.com Perspectives on Beauty.

A Sailing Family

"The place of the father in the modern suburban family is a
very small one, particularly if he plays golf." (Or sails?)
Bertrand Russell

"The family is one of nature's masterpieces."
George Santayana

"Having children makes you no more a parent
than having a piano makes you a pianist."
Michael Levine

"To nourish children and raise them against odds is
in any time, any place, more valuable than to
fix bolts in cars or design nuclear weapons"
Marilyn French.

My dream was to have a sailing family. The sailboat would be a microcosm of togetherness. We would learn teamwork and individual responsibility. We would learn how each person is dependent on the others. We would explore and discover. They would learn to love the unknown, to glory in the warm sun and the fresh breezes, to anticipate the cool swim. We would grow closer as a family and appreciate each other more fully. And, of course, the captain was in charge! A bonus for the father figure!

They would learn how to trim sails, read charts, predict the weather. Their eyes would look east and wonder what lands lay on the other side. They would meet other sailing families, make new friends from other places, exchange stories, explore ports and islands together. They would dream dreams of their own boats and voyages.

When I purchased *Cygnet* in 1979, I had four children: Donna, 20; David, 18; Debra 17 and Dara, 14. *Cygnet* could sleep only five and was a tight fit for a family of six, so family sails were mostly day sails. The first part of the dream had to be modified; cruising would be with only part of the family. It also was more practical. The schedules for college and teenage children were difficult to mesh.

Figure 34 Son David, a natural sailor.

The first summer I felt we made a great start. Everyone went day sailing on the Hudson River several times. We sailed north to Bear Mountain Bridge where the river narrows, the current runs swiftly and the depth is 175 feet, and south to the Tappan Zee Bridge, where the river is wider. Haverstraw Bay is three miles across. The tide pushes north as far as Albany, nearly 150 miles upstream. The Hudson River was our day sailing area. We encountered all types of sailing conditions and even dared to swim in the river. Pollution was diminishing. Long absent fish were returning. Fish from the river could be eaten safely as often as once a week.

Our first cruise was exciting to anticipate. The crew was Donna, her college friend, Mary, and new friends who loved to sail, Jack and Maryjean. We sailed down the Hudson, under the George Washington Bridge with its little red light house on the Manhattan shore, past the Statue of Liberty, and up the East River. We looked down the canyons of cross streets of Manhattan, kept pace with joggers, and met tugboats pushing barges.

Our first crises came as we passed under the Whitestone Bridge. The one-cylinder Marstal engine was coughing and dying. It would start, run briefly, and stop. When I had the boat surveyed for insurance coverage, the surveyor stipulated that the gas tank had to be converted from a bottom feed with its risk of gasoline leakage into the bilge and a disasterous explosion, to a top feed. Gasoline was fed by natural flow. In making the change, I installed a low-pressure gas pump. However, it was pumping too much gas and choking the engine. As we emerged into Long Island Sound, another sailor, hearing and seeing our predicament, offered us his mooring in Little Neck Bay. He would go on a friend's empty mooring. It is another example of how sailors look out for one another. We gratefully accepted.

The next day, we motored with a sputtering engine to City Island and Minneford's, an old-line shipyard that built mine sweepers during World War II and America's Cup winners earlier. I was fearful we might have to abandon the cruise. A mechanic quickly diagnosed the problem, installed a rubber primer pump like those used with outboard motor tanks, and disconnected the pump. We were on our way again. We simply primed the engine by hand to start. Then the gas fed normally and only occasionally did we have to pump while running.

The cruise out the Sound was exciting as we explored ports new to us: Oyster Bay, Port Jefferson with its gunk hole, Mattituck winding up a creek about three miles to open into a small harbor. We climbed the high sand dunes of the gunk hole and looked back at the village and out across the lake. (See chapter one for episode in Gardner Bay during this cruise.) We visited Coeckle's Harbor on Shelter Island and Greenport on the north fork.

My hopes and expectations were all being met. The boat was seaworthy, sailed well, and was comfortable. The crew was terrific. Donna and I had new-shared experiences and we got to know each other better. It was the beginning of a long friendship with Jack and Maryjean and many sailing adventures.

Unexpected Crew

For the cruise the next year, I wanted one of the other children to go. I told Dara, 15, she could invite anyone she wanted. I was thinking of a girl friend. She invited her guitar teacher, a good-looking young man of 26! The decision was tough. I hadn't made any stipulations on whom she could ask. Yet, if there was a particle of romance there, would I be encouraging and enhancing it? The boat was small. Donna, Dara's older sister, and my friend Jack, were the other crew-members. There would not be much opportunity for surreptious romance in that crowded setting. I conferred with her mother and we decided to proceed. It soon became apparent romantic electricity was not sizzling. It was simply a friendship!

We were sailing from *Cygnet's* homeport in Haverstraw, NY on the Hudson River above the Tappan Zee Bridge and heading out Long Island Sound. It meant sailing down the Hudson River, around Manhattan, out the East River and into the Long Island Sound.

The second day was hot and humid. *Cygnet* had no dodger, no relief from the sun; there was no shade on the boat except forward behind the sail. Dara was becoming uncomfortable. A poison ivy rash began to appear and it itched unmercifully. She was miserable. Her only relief was to go overboard to allow the cool, salt water to sooth her skin. She hung on a rope and trailed behind the boat, got out to warm up, and then back into the water again.

Our port was Oyster Bay. We got in a little after 8:00 p.m. and tied up to a dock. Dara and Kevin went looking for a drug store to find medication that would stop the itching. They arrived just after closing time at 9:00 p.m. A supermarket was open nearby but had nothing. They were standing outside the store discussing possible options when a small, elderly woman stopped, having overhead their frustration and dilemma. She said, *"I'll drive you to an open drug store. It's only a short distance. But first I must tell my family what I'm doing."* Dara and Kevin followed her to her car. It was an older Rolls Royce. They got in and within a few minutes they were entering a gated estate. They traveled back dirt roads, through estate properties, and heard stories about the Roosevelts (Theodore had a summer place on Oyster Bay). They were back on board by 10:30 p.m. with some medication. Her gifts of help and concern were gratefully received.

However, the medication did not help. The poison ivy was spreading over her body. She spent a restless, uncomfortable and sleepless night. She was miserable. My great plan to introduce her to cruising was going seriously awry.

We weighed anchor and got away early from Oyster Bay. Again, it was a blistering hot day. The poison ivy continued to spread. Even a swimming suit was uncomfortable. The only relief was cool salt water flowing over her body as she trailed on a line behind the boat. It slowed us, but was necessary.

We arrived in Port Jefferson after dinner. Dara decided she wanted to abandon ship. But we were a hundred miles from home. The options were a train into Manhattan and a bus to Rockland County, her mother driving to Port Jeff through heavy traffic, or a ferry. The ferry runs between Port Jefferson and Bridgeport, CT. and would be a much easier drive. A telephone call to her mother, Ann, and arrangements were made. Dara was on the ferry the next morning. It was her first and last long cruise with her Dad although there were many shorter sails. Her guitar teacher elected to stay for the rest of the cruise.

One of the highlights of the cruise came in Coeckles Harbor on Shelter Island. The entrance is narrow but opens up into a bay that leads back to a very protected harbor. We were tied up at a dock and had finished dinner. Kevin got his guitar out and began playing. A few minutes later, the captain of a large motor yacht next to us across the dock began playing along with Kevin. We ended up on the aft deck of his yacht, playing and singing. Jack, a drummer and band member in a previous life, found a boat surface to drum on. It was one of the serendipitous moments of sailing. Good food for the soul. Friendship. Natural beauty. Music. A starlit night to remember.

Heavy Fog

Block Island was sunny and warm. *Wind Dancer* was anchored in the Great Salt Pond. Jack, Maryjean, and my daughter Debbie had sailed from City Island. We rented bicycles, toured and circled the island. We stopped at the old lighthouse on Monhegan Bluffs, endangered because of the erosion of the bluffs. The lighthouse was first lit in 1875 and became automatic in 1990. New Shoreham was incorporated in 1672 on Block, the smallest town in Rhode Island.

We biked along the southern shore and stopped to climb down the steep, high dunes to a sandy beach below. The ocean was in heavy fog; the island was sunny. We continued to bike to Gay Head on the southwest corner of the island. On a sunny day one could see for miles.

The next morning, we awoke to an opera soloist singing an aria from La Traviata. The Italian bakery on the Island delivered fresh bread and breakfast rolls to visiting boaters. The baker sang his way from boat to boat. We eagerly bought some sticky buns.

We weighed anchor and headed for the channel. As we approached, we could see the first channel marker but the second and third markers were hidden in fog. We turned around and anchored again. Another day on Block. Jack and Maryjean were planning to get off at Cutty Hunk, but because of work schedules decided they would take the ferry from Block to the mainland.

Debbie and I cleaned the boat, swam, lunched, and walked to Old Harbor on the other side of the island. The harbor is small, mostly populated with fishing boats. The ferry to the mainland also docks there. We browsed in gift shops, snacked, and killed time. We decided that we were leaving the next day if we could see the buoys to guide us out through the channel.

The sea fog in the harbor quickly dissipated. But the fog on the ocean hung low. We raised a radar reflector high into the rigging so other boats and ships could see us more easily. We would be crossing the ferry route and channels into Narragansett Bay where ships were going to and coming from Providence, RI.

We fired up the diesel, hauled up the anchor and motored to the channel. Upon reaching the first marker, we could just make out the second, and as we proceeded, the third. We were going out, heading for Cutty Hunk Island.

Not only was there fog, but also the currents are tricky. When the tide is rising and the ocean water is rushing inland, it goes north into Narragansett Bay, west into Long Island Sound and east into Buzzards Bay. If your timing is right, you can ride the current east when the tide is going out, and pick up an eastern current when it is coming in, boosting your speed throughout the day. If you miss, you can be bucking current both ways, dramatically increasing travel time. A two-knot current against as opposed to with us meant a difference of four nautical miles per hour. It would dramatically increase our sailing time. But our timing was good.

The fog was so thick that you could see only three or four boat lengths. There was no wind and we were under power. We blasted the air horn to let other boats know we were there. We listened intently, sometimes shutting the engine down so we could hear better. Sound in fog can behave in strange ways. Fog can dampen down the sound of the signal. The danger may be closer than the sound proposes. Conversely, the signal may be loud but still at a great distance. In short, they are a good warning, but not reliable in terms of distance and even direction. We were surprised when a sailboat under power came out of the fog directly ahead of us. We had not heard them.

As we approached the northern tip of Block Island, we knew we had to stay outside the treacherous shoals. They were marked by a buoy on the water and a lighthouse on land. Our Loran guided us directly to the buoy and we left it on our starboard.

Now we were approaching the ferry route. We listened intently for its foghorn and engines. Often the low rumble of the diesel engines carry through the fog as effectively as the foghorn.

There it was! The foghorn! How far we could not tell. It was on our starboard. Was the ferry coming towards us or away from us? We waited tensely for the next signal, strained to hear the sound of the engines, watched warily for the emergence of a huge bow, ready to sound our air horn and to take evasive action. We could turn sharply away, increase engine power and speed, blow our horn repeatedly. But it likely would not be heard. Nor would we be seen. Avoiding a collision would be up to us! The next signal was to our port. It had passed ahead of us and was now moving away from us!

Within the next hour, the fog began to clear and the wind began to freshen. We raised sails and turned off the engine. We were moving well with the current. The crisis was over. We would see our good friends, John and Carmen, on Cutty Hunk. John taught at the Boston University School of Theology and pastored the little church on the island in the summers.

I admired Debbie for her calm. She did not panic. We learned more about each other, daughter and father. She was a good companion and good crew. Unfortunately, sailing did not turn out to be her love. Nausea interfered, as did tense and scary moments. She preferred her soul nourishment in some other form. My plan for family togetherness was not working out. Only Donna became an avid sailor and a frequent sailing companion. And for that, I am grateful.

An Unexpected Gift

Nieces and nephews grow up, get married, have families and live long distances away. It is difficult on tight budgets and busy schedules to find time to get to know each other. Therefore, I was delighted when my niece Jan wrote that she and her husband would like to sail.

Jan and Dan lived in San Diego. Dan was in the submarine service and would spend six months most years away from his family. He decided he needed to be a full-time dad to his boys and retired from the Navy. They were a "water family," involved in competitive water skiing. While not sailors, they were at home on boats and comfortable on the water.

We sailed the Bay of Quinte on Lake Ontario, a kind of inland passage inside the north shore. We ate very well with Jan's planning and cooking: blackened steaks, corn on the cob, and green salad. Every night a different menu. We enjoyed hikes in Picton with its beautiful homes and a jazz concert on the dock in Belleville. We motored through the Murray Canal and dropped toll money into a cup that was extended out over the water on the end of a pole. A "miss" and the process had to be repeated with the cost doubled.

We endured swarming shadflies when we anchored behind Wapoos Island and motored out through shallows by aligning ourselves with a straight road that ran down a steep hill to the harbor. It was a time of getting acquainted, more together time in a week than most relationships get in a year. We discovered we really liked each other.

Figure 35 On another trip through the Murray Canal, Sophie deposits the toll in the extended collection cup. Photo by Jean Finlayson-Schueler.

The Grandchild Plot

My grandchildren range in age from two to twenty. They came in every way: naturally, by marriage and by adoption—14 in all! Six boys and eight girls. Caucasian, Eurasian, Chinese and Vietnamese.

Figure 36 Grandchildren Sarah and Daniel—hang on! Photo by the author.

Figure 37 Grandchildren Brienne, Zack, Daniel and Sarah—very 'at home' on *Wind Dancer.* Photo by the author.

Figure 38 Grandson Daniel getting the feel of the boat. Photo by the author.

Figure 39 SadieGrace and her Aunt Deb underway. Photo by the author.

Figure 40 Donna getting SadieGrace started at an early age. Photo by
the author.

Figure 41 Sadie and her Dad Ken. Photo by the author.

Figure 42 Lissa on a cruise with her granddad. Photo by the author.

Figure 43 Delainey and her mom underway.

Figure 44 Delainey—lifejackets are a requirement when in the cockpit or on deck. Photo by the author.

I've devised a more devious plan for them. For several years we have rented a house on Lake Ontario. It has a big front yard for land games, and a stair step set of flat rocks into the water. Toddlers can wade and the older ones can swim. I figure that if I put them in the environment, they'll warm up to it like I did as a kid.

Wind Dancer is at the Henderson Harbor Yacht Club just five minutes down the road. We bring her into the dock and the kids swim and jump off her. We go out for short day sails. The older ones love to be towed behind the boat, and to be rescued if we get going too fast and they can't hold on. They're learning to be comfortable around boats and in the water, and confident they'll be rescued if they go overboard. We get them on the boat as infants, as toddlers, as pre-schoolers.

We will pull up behind some land in the bay, drop the anchor, and let the kids swim off the boat. They like balancing on the stern or bow pulpits and jumping or diving in. Under sail, they learn to steer and see how the boat handles, that it is not all a mystery. I enrolled several in the yacht club sailing school where they "learn the ropes" with their peers and on small boats.

The results are not all in yet. But there is progress. And there is hope that this generation can feel *"the bliss"* of sailing, find the challenge, discover the mystery, appreciate the natural world and all its beauty. My hope and prayer is that they will find that sailing is one of the ways they can nurture their spirits.

Batting 200

My batting average for getting my family enchanted with sailing is not great. My hope was that the average would increase when I married Barbara. We sailed quite a lot together. We sailed out of Boston to Provincetown on the Cape, through the Cape Cod Canal, to Martha's Vineyard and Nantucket. We sailed Long Island Sound, Buzzards Bay, visited Block Island, Nantucket and Cutty Hunk.

On Lake Ontario Barbara and I have sailed the length of the lake, through the Canadian Bay of Quinte, through the Thousand Islands. We entertained many guests in day sails and overnights. We traveled to Kingston and Gananoque, Ontario where we enjoy the lively towns and excellent restaurants.

She has become an expert sailor. She can raise the sails, trim the sails, and reef the sails. She can read charts and plot courses. But she doesn't like to sail! She was doing it just for me. Will power does not seem to work in love or in love of sailing.

She often gets nauseous. She's tried everything from wrist bracelets to patches to pills. Some knock her out. Others simply don't work. She also has a deathly fear of water. When she was eight, she almost drowned. She still carries that trauma with her while she works to exorcise it through therapy. She has become more comfortable on the boat but still finds too much heeling uncomfortable. And she is very fearful of my going overboard and she not being able to rescue me. I do all the forward bow and sail work in rough seas. More rescue practice might help.

Barbara tends to remember the worst and scariest times on board. I tend to remember the good times, the exhilarating sails, the camaraderie, the new places, the companionship. From my perspective, we've had some wonderful times. From Barbara's, it's been grit, grin and bear it. To paraphrase Michael Levine, a family owning a sailboat doesn't make a sailing family.

In looking back over the hundreds of miles Barbara and I have sailed together, I am humbled by her love. She overrode fear, terror, seasickness, and boredom to sail with her husband. In the first years, she hid it well. I was not aware of the terror and the dread.

As I reflect on her gift, it occurs to me that there is more than one way "to give one's life for a friend (or a husband)." We give our lives through our presence in another's life, through quality time, through sharing the journey and seeing the joy our presence brings to the other. It is a gift that reaches into the soul.

◆   ◆   ◆

The quotations by Bertrand Russell, George Santayana, Michael Levine and Marilyn French are from www.wisdomquotes.com. Jone Johnson Lewis. 2006. (http://www.wisdomquotes.com/cat_beauty.html)

In Conclusion

"Life is a succession of lessons, which must be lived to be understood ..."
Ralph Waldo Emerson

*"Life is many things at different times ... from interesting, exciting, surprising
and challenging, to frustrating, discouraging and stressful.
But we learn from every experience, good or bad, and move on from there."*
Barbara Brabec

"There is more to life than increasing its speed."
Mahatma Ghandi

When I was working in New York City, I often traveled to other cities. As my flight neared New York, I found myself gearing up, getting ready for the faster pace of the city. It was like I had to get my wheels rolling at the same speed as the pressure-paced city. Walking faster. Keeping up with traffic. Rushing into the subway station and onto a train. If you didn't keep up, you got run over or run down. It wasn't a negative experience. It was just the way it was.

In sailing, I found I could slow down. I didn't have to move at an ever "increasing speed." I had time to enjoy the sunsets, to feel the warm sun on my skin, the breeze in my face, to enjoy God's creation. There was time for conversation and meditation, time for friendship and conversation. There was the excitement of new places—and the excitement of fantastic sails. There were the challenges of the unexpected.

I've discovered that words of encouragement or simply listening—can change a person's life. Often I ask myself, *"If I don't do this, will I regret it later?"* It helps me make positive decisions for my life. And I try to affirm the good in me and in others, and distance myself from affirming the darker side of our natures. I look for nourishing, healthy food for my soul. When I fall off my soul-food diet, I find myself slipping, languishing.

In a real sense, *Wind Dancer* became a "sacred space," a place of healing and renewal, a place for the nourishing of the soul. At one point of distress in my life, a time of depression and hopelessness, I found healing in worship. Liturgies that once seemed dry of inspiration came alive because I was in a different place. I've found healing and energy during walks in the woods or at night in a canoe on a quiet lake. I urge you to find your place—your sacred space—where you can find healing and hope and energy.

You might set your "spirit sails" to catch the refreshing breezes of renewal that carry you into a new or deeper relationship with that entity—that holy essence—we call God, Allah, the Almighty, or the Great Spirit.

Emerson, Ralph Waldo. www.WisdomQuotes.com. 2004
Brabec, Barbara. www.barbarabrabex.com/lifelessonslearned.htm, 2004.
Ghandi, Mahatma. www.leadershipdevelopment.com/html/quotations3.php.2004

After Word—Life Lessons

Sailing often teaches lessons that carry over into other areas of our lives. Many have been chronicled in previous chapters. The following lessons didn't fit into those chapter categories but bear considering. I learned them through experience, not books. Some were learned through poor judgment. Others are lighter and sometimes humorous. Here are some I've learned.

Check Landmarks—Your Progress may not be what you think it is.

The day was clear, sun bright, wind light. We were traveling west through the East River approaching Manhattan. We passed LaGuardia Airport with planes seeming almost to clip the top of our mast. We passed Typhoid Mary's Island, a deserted host to a former sanatorium. We turned southwest towards Hell Gate, the juncture of the East and Harlem Rivers. Sailboats cannot traverse the Harlem and take a short cut to the Hudson River because of low bridges. Tall masted boats must go down the East River past the eastside of Manhattan to New York Harbor.

As we approached the power plant and the railroad bridge, *Cygnet* was handling well. The wind was light but filling her sails. She responded to the tiller. Water was flowing past the hull and rudder. It was quiet and serene.

After ten minutes or so, our progress seemed minimal. We checked the shore. We actually were slowly moving backwards. The current was stronger against us than the wind was powerful with us. We needed additional power if we were to make progress. The "iron sail"—the motor—was the answer. We began to move forward again.

Life Lesson: Everything may seem to be going well on your job, in the community organization, or in the neighborhood if you consider only the internal factors. If you look outside at other benchmarks, you may find your boat slipping back, slipping behind, and additional power or energy may be needed.

Communicate with your crew

Sailing out of Nantucket Harbor, the wind was from the west. Normally we would sail west through narrow shoaled channels to Martha's Vineyard and southwest through Vineyard Sound. But the day was pretty, the sun was out, and the breeze was fresh. There were two of us on board. Barbara, my wife, was a novice sailor at that time.

I decided we would go outside into the open Atlantic, down the east side of Nantucket Island, then head for Block Island. The winds, if they stayed where they were, would give us a beam reach, an easy sail.

The sail by Nantucket was beautiful. The sky was clear, the sun was warm, and the wind was fresh. The boat was moving easily. We spotted several large commercial fishing vessels and a few sport-fishing boats. As we neared the tip of Nantucket, fog began to roll in. Visibility became a few hundred feet. When we cleared the island, we headed towards Block, sailing over the Nantucket shoals. I was watching the depth finder for shoaling. Water depth was a steady 12-15 feet. We drew six feet. Charts indicated a uniform depth but I didn't want any surprises. We felt alone out there in the fog.

I asked Barbara to keep an eye out for other boats. Visibility should allow us maneuvering time if sighted. And we would certainly hear their engines before we saw them. I was thinking of the sport fishing boats. Barbara was thinking of large freighters emerging out of the fog and smashing into us. I knew they wouldn't be in the shoal water. She didn't. She was terrified.

In the meantime, the wind had shifted. We changed our course from Block Island to Martha's Vineyard. We did not emerge from the fog until we sighted Gay Head on Martha's Vineyard in late afternoon. Barbara was tense and scared the whole day. But she didn't say, and I didn't know.

We proceeded to an anchorage in quiet waters in the channel between Nashawena and Pasque Islands, two of the Elizabeth Island chain that drops down from the Cape. The channel connects Vineyard Sound with Buzzards Bay.

When Barbara and I were safely anchored, we talked about the day. I discovered again my lack of communication and how I could have eased her fear and pain. It was a day of agony for her, a day of watchfulness for me, but not life threatening.

Life lesson: Communicate with your family, work colleagues, friends, and sailing crew. Let them know what your plans are, what the risks are, what emergency plans can be put into place, what they can do to ensure their own safety.

The Captain is always responsible, regardless

Sailing at night is often delightful. We were sailing towards Provincetown on Cape Cod from Boston. The wind was light. We were under power and sail, moving at over 6 ½ knots. The sea was relatively calm. We were protected from the waves by the hook of the Cape, moving towards a bell marker off Long Point. Upon reaching the marker, we would turn northeast into Provincetown harbor. The wind was coming across the port side of the boat. We were flying the main and the large genoa that swept along the deck almost back to the cockpit.

Bob and Lou were below, cleaning up the galley and the main cabin after a late evening meal. I was busy on deck and in the cockpit tidying up and preparing for anchoring. I had given the helmsperson a compass heading towards the marker. Bob had suggested she head for the light on the marker. She was sticking to the heading religiously.

Tiring, the helmsperson sat down. She lost sight of the light. It disappeared behind the genoa sail. She sailed by the compass heading. From under the sail, a large object appeared. *"Where did that come from?"* she said, turning the wheel sharply. But it was too late. We hit with a glancing blow. Was it another boat? A floating object? A large log? A container that fell off a fishing boat? No, it was the marker, a large steel buoy rising above the deck of the boat. Although floating, it was an immoveable object. The chances of hitting a marker, even though steering towards it, are remote. It's a small target in a big expanse of water.

Bob checked immediately for water below. The hull had not been penetrated. I went forward with a flashlight to inspect the outside of the hull. There was a gouge high up near the rub rail but it had not pierced through the hull. The steersperson was shaken, frightened, crying, and guilt-ridden. Bob took the helm. We talked. We were in one piece, the rigging was standing and undamaged, and no one was injured. We proceeded into the harbor and anchored for the night, tired and relieved.

The next morning, in the warm sun, I repaired the gouge in the hull. It would need some cosmetic finishing upon completion of the cruise, but no permanent damage had been done. The temporary repair would keep moisture from entering into the exposed fiberglass.

Life lesson: Regardless of who is steering, or who is charting, or who is the lookout, the captain is ultimately responsible for the safety of the ship and its passengers. So is the chief executive of any corporation. That does not mean micromanagement. It means macro oversight.

Caution, sometimes, is the best course

The captain was taking a poll of his three-member crew. Should we stay on the ocean or head for the Intracoastal Waterway? Four of us, I was crew, were sailing from Cape Canaveral, Florida to Annapolis, Maryland on a 42-foot ketch. We were approaching a decision point as to whether to go around the treacherous

Cape Hatteras—many ships had foundered on her shoals—or go to the safer inside passage, the Intracoastal Waterway.

Each day at 4:00 p.m., we checked with our weather advisor by radio. He was in touch with boats up and down the East Coast, out to Bermuda, down into the Caribbean. He read the national weather reports, tracked the fronts, estimated their arrival times and the ocean conditions. Because he had reports from many locations—boats that were on the water and reporting actual weather conditions—he had a better fix on the weather than the national services.

He informed us that a major front was coming through with powerful winds. Furthermore, it was to be followed shortly by two additional lows. We would not get out of stormy weather for five days or until we reached Cape May, N.J. We elected to head for Beaufort, N.C. to our northwest. It was about 36 hours away. We had moved fairly far offshore.

The crew stood three hour shifts twice a day—the same time period day or night. My shift was 11:00 to 2:00. We were nearing Beaufort during the night shift, sighting lighthouses, and checking GPS position. Making landfall in early morning was so exciting that I slept only two hours of the 36-hour trip. Yet, I felt little fatigue, the adrenalin was pumping strongly.

We made Beaufort without incident. On the Intracoastal, however, we experienced the full fury of the storm. Rain was so heavy and so driving that it hurt your eyes to keep them open. Markers in the narrow channel disappeared. The wind swept across the open bay and pushed at us, seemingly trying to shove us aground. But we were thankful we were not on the open water, facing huge waves, driving rain, and 50-60 knot winds.

Life lesson: It is sometimes wise to heed the danger signs and to steer a safer course. It also is wise to have competent advisors—the radioman monitoring weather reports and conditions—to warn against very risky conditions.

It Ain't Always As It Appears

The clothes washing detergent was under the sink in the galley in a large Arm&Hammer gallon jug. There was a change of crew at Niagara-on-the-Lake. Towels, sheets and clothes needed washing.

I had sailed over with one crew, my sister Helen from Florida and her daughter, Chris from Oregon. We sailed out of Oswego, NY at the east end of the Lake, along the American side of Lake Ontario, then hopped across to the Canadian ports of Whitby and Toronto. We were meeting Barbara, my wife, at Niagara-on-the-Lake, near the west end. She drove cross-state from Syracuse and her family flew and drove in from Tennessee and Ohio. It is a small and beautiful

Canadian town at the mouth of the Niagara River as it flows north from the Niagara Falls into Lake Ontario. The west side of the river is Canadian; the east side U.S. With a population of about 15,000, it hosts over a million visitors a year for its Shaw Festival of plays by Shaw and other playwrights of that era.

There was a two-day layover for theatre, restaurants, shopping, and viewing of the always-spectacular Canadian Falls. This time the sun was shining brightly and mist from the falls rose above the cliffs where we stood. The water from four of the Great Lakes was tumbling over the falls, draining down the Niagara River into Lake Ontario and ultimately out the St. Lawrence River to the Atlantic Ocean. Two rainbows rose above the water into the mist, the "pot o'gold" just a few yards away but so inaccessible. No matter how many times one sees the falls, the scene of the water rushing over the rock ledge into the river below is awesome. The water has come from rivers and streams in Canada, Minnesota, Wisconsin, Illinois, Indiana, Michigan, Pennsylvania and New York. The lakes comprise one-fifth of the world's fresh water surface.

Back at the boat, we piled the laundry in plastic bags, grabbed the detergent from under the sink, and took off for the Laundromat. We had two loads and I poured the detergent into each washer, pushed the coins in and started the wash. We passed the time by reading.

Finally, the wash cycle was finished. I opened the lid and pulled out the damp clothes. To my surprise, there were dark splotches on the towels. I pulled out more clothes. Sheets, an orange outfit of my sister's, other clothes—everything looked like a poor job of tie-dye!

My first reaction was, *"What's wrong with these machines?"* Then Barbara said, *"Let me see that detergent!"* I unscrewed the cap and she held the jug up to her nose. It curled up and her face spoke loudly. *"It's oil!"* she said. The light slowly dawned. I had pumped the dirty crank case oil out of the engine into the detergent jug in the Fall when I changed the oil and winterized the engine—and hadn't labeled it. I forgot I hadn't taken it to the recycle barrel at the marina. What was in the jug wasn't detergent—but dirty oil!

I went to the supermarket for real detergent and Shout to try get the stains out in a second wash. I scrubbed at the dark blobs. Barbara, looking at Helen's spoiled outfit, said I would need to buy her a new one. At the end of the second wash, the stains were less but still prominent. It would take several washes to remove the stains, if at all. We put the wash in the dryer and went back to the boat with a poor imitation of tie-dyed clothes. Helen was a good sport and said she'd gotten the outfit at bargain prices, not to worry. We all had a good laugh—especially when we shared it with the others—and the story is sure to live for several years.

Life lesson: Even reasonably intelligent people goof up—and a sense of humor helps move us through our stupid mistakes.

As with most every boat, *Wind Dancer* has many sea stories, a virtual sea chest full of adventure and romance, if only she could reveal all she has seen and experienced. It would be a different tale but one full of spirit and the spiritual.

About the Author of Spirit Sail

◆

Nelson Price

Nelson Price has been involved in media his entire career as executive, writer and producer. Most recently he served as president and CEO of the *Odyssey Television Channel*, now the *Hallmark Channel*. Odyssey was launched in 1987 as an interfaith cable network to present programs of faith, values and spirituality. The network presented programs featuring Nelson Mandella (his first appearance in the U.S. after his release from prison), Tony Campolo, President and Mrs. Clinton, Archbishop Tutu, and Ellie Wiesel among dozens of others.

The National Interfaith Cable Coalition, with 68 denominations and religious organizations as members, sponsored the network. Protestant, Catholic, Orthodox, and Jewish groups were represented. Price also served as NICC president and CEO. It was the largest interfaith organization in the country.

Earlier Price served as a communications officer for the United Methodist Church nationally with offices in New York City. He shot documentary films in China, India, Africa and the U.S. He was executive producer of an eight-part series on "endings and beginnings" that aired on most PBS stations. Entitled *Begin with Goodbye*," the thesis was that in order to move on in life after a tragic loss, one had to say "goodbye." Losses included death, loss of a part of one's body, terminal illness, divorce, children leaving home and moving, among others. Screen and stage actor Eli Wallach hosted.

In radio, Price was executive producer of the first national radio call-in program, *Night Call*. It aired each weekday night on a network of over 100 radio stations in rural to urban markets. Special equipment had to be designed to handle a three-way conversation on air at that time. The program launched immediately following the assassination of Dr. Martin Luther King, Jr. to "help heal a tormented nation." Callers interacted with the host, Del Shields, and a prominent guest, persons who ranged from Bill Cosby to Black Panther leaders. As many as 40,000 calls were placed to the program in a single night.

In the 1970's there was great concern over the effects of television violence on children. Price was one of the founders and served as President/CEO of the Media Action Research Center, Inc. Dr. Robert Liebert, a professor at the State University of New York at Stony Brook, was the scientific director. Children were tested in a MARC laboratory to determine the effects of both violent and pro-social TV scenes. Results of the research were presented to congressional committees. A curriculum was developed, *Television Awareness Training*, to train teachers and parents about the social effects of television on children and adults.

His sailing started in Chicago on Lake Michigan and continued when he moved to New York. He has sailed on the Great lakes and the Atlantic Ocean in boats ranging from 25 to 50 feet. He sailed out of homeports on the Hudson River, City Island in New York City, Chicago and Lake Ontario. His cruising has taken him to most ports on Long Island Sound and to Block Island, Newport, Martha's Vineyard, Nantucket, Cape Cod, Boston, Portsmouth and Maine. He has traveled the IntraCoastal Waterway and sailed from Cape Canaveral to Annapolis. In 1988, Price received a captain's license from the United States Coast Guard as master for vessels up to 50 tons. While a recreational sailor, Price has accumulated over four years "before the mast."

In both his work and his sailing, Price has been on a spiritual journey. *Spirit Sail* is a part of that adventure.

Price has four adult children and 14 grandchildren. He is married to Barbara Croll Fought, a professor of law and broadcast journalism at Syracuse University.

Visit www.spiritual-sailing com

978-0-595-46327-5
0-595-46327-4

Printed in the United States
109512LV00002B/199/A